ok may

W9-AFC-819

DIVINE
PERFECTION

DIVINE

PERFECTION

possible ideas of God

BY FREDERICK SONTAG

HARPER & BROTHERS

PUBLISHERS

NEW YORK

For

C.N.S. and M.B.S.

PREFACE

What should a man do if he finds himself outside and unable to identify with any of the major philosophical and theological trends of his time? If he should happen to be interested in speculative and constructive work, then to turn to and concentrate upon any one historical figure or era is too confining and misses the aim. For any constructive effort every previous theory is relevant, although all not equally so. To make every major theory (although not all of history à la Hegel) your training ground—what a fantastic but necessary procedure!

British thought, both positivistic and analytic, is highly specialized, often doctrinaire, and sometimes provincial. Admirable as its aims and methods may be at points, it seems unsuited to speculative efforts. It may criticise them effectively, but it appears unable to create them. On the other hand, German thought has been so fruitful that its products are hard to avoid. Yet from the critical thought of Kant to the towers of Hegel and the humanism of Feuerbach and Nietzsche, it seems to have spent its creative energy. To stir its fire will renew the heat of any mind which has a speculative bent; but, if it is time for a change, this seems hardly the place to turn.

If one of our problems is the modern split between philosophy and theology, then to leap with others onto the existentialist bandwagon might appear to be the answer. In existentialism we have at once a philosophical, theological, and literary movement, plus a revival of classical ontological problems. Yet for all this, it is hard to remember that existentialism actually is of nineteenth-century

7

origin. Its literary flowering and public attention are recent, but its basis lies before our time. Furthermore, it avowedly aims at a radical break with its immediate past, if not with the past as a whole. What seems most needed today is new theorizing on fundamental problems, theorizing which seems to be *from* the tradition rather than *against* it. We cannot go back; somehow we must bring all past metaphysical and theological writing to us and enlist its aid toward constructing contemporary theories.

At Stanford University, where I first saw the light and was converted to the use of the philosophic method, my thanks must go to Lawrence Kimpton, John Mothershead (who first made me anxious to read all previous philosophy), John Reid, and Jeffery Smith. Outside philosophy's door, Graham DuShane and Virgil Whitaker taught me what a teacher did and still could do. Those were exciting postwar days for a product of the California public schools.

I was told, and it was true, that nowhere outside New Haven would it be so possible or so fruitful to work both in theology and in philosophy. In my own era as a graduate student at Yale this seemed uniquely true. As a trio of teachers, Brand Blanshard, Robert Calhoun, and Paul Weiss were and are and probably will be an unbeatable combination. Whatever clarity and directness are here, Blanshard may take credit for if he will. A love of classical theories and a desire to reproduce them without distortion—both are from Calhoun, although they are not equal to him. Sheer speculative construction and daring, a confidence in one's own theories—these no one could fail to learn from Weiss. Philosophy was as it ought to be there, so that my debt in this essay is to the whole Department, including, of course, Julian Hartt (with whom I first worked on the problem of this essay) and Albert Outler at the Divinity School. The students there taught too, by making you feel that you were in the right competition. Those years produced a dedication to philosophy as an instrument, an openness to every past and present theory, as well as the beginning of an interest in the subject of this essay.

Nine years as a teacher of philosophy to Pomona College students made me into a writer. The faculty and the College as a whole provide a uniquely free and congenial atmosphere, and the students encourage you by finding speculation natural and traditional questions both relevant and urgently to be dealt with. Actually, the draft of this essay was completed in New York City, in a small room in Butler Library, provided for me by the generosity of the Columbia University Department of Philosophy, while I was across Broadway as a Visiting Professor of Philosophy at Union Theological Seminary during 1959–1960. Although I had taken seminars in theology at Yale, I had never actually been in or been a part of a Seminary before, and that year at Union must stand as one of my most instructive and fruitful. The faculty and students were more than generous to a philosophical Philistine, but they must also bear part of the responsibility for orienting my philosophical writing toward theological problems.

John Bennett, Reinhold Niebuhr, Cyril Richardson, and Daniel Williams were all kind enough to read the draft of this essay in detail and must not go without public thanks. I have profited from their comments and conversation, even if the manuscript may not reveal it. Without the secretarial office at Union the rough draft would not have been done. Without Mrs. Carol Ehman the final draft would not have been done nearly as well. Through all of this my wife patiently read and corrected what she protested she did not understand. If the reader's experience is otherwise, no little credit is due to her.

Claremont, California   F.S.
November, 1961

CONTENTS

DIVINE
PERFECTION

PART ONE

SEVEN

TYPES

OF

DIVINE

PERFECTION

INTRODUCTION TO PART ONE

In our own time not only philosophers but also theologians often seem unwilling to speak directly, clearly, and (most important) simply about the nature of God. This was not always so, and it need not be so in the future. Much, of course, has been written about the difficulty of arriving at any certain knowledge of the Divine nature. However, theoretical difficulties do not seem to have diminished interest in the subject. How can we develop further the widespread contemporary interest in theology without a constant attempt to delineate the nature of God as precisely as possible and in technical and philosophically adequate terms?

To some it may seem strange to assert that there is currently little direct discussion about the Divine nature, when everywhere these days one hears a great deal about God and about religious concepts. Yet much talk about religion or extended discussion about God's action, however comprehensive it may be, is not the same as metaphysical and systematic investigation of the Divine attributes. And such metaphysical elaboration is important precisely because we are not always clear or in agreement as to how God acts or as to the role He plays in any particular religion. Disagreements at this level, as classical theology knew full well, often rest upon a fundamental diversity in the way in which we conceive God's nature and His attributes.

A systematic inquiry, then, need not attempt to arrive at a single,

17

definitive, and universally acceptable description of the basic qualities which constitute a conception of God, but it should aim to clarify the basis of our disagreement over God's actions by setting forth the varying concepts of God's nature as metaphysically conceived (i.e., by a description of the interrelating basic attributes of such a primary nature). In this way we might see why, in virtue of His nature, God is conceived to act in one way by some and in another way by others. And it is possible to avoid the epistemological problems which have made theologians and metaphysicians intellectually shy in the presence of the task of describing God. For if we view such an enterprise not as one providing conclusive knowledge, but rather as an undertaking which will enable us to see more clearly why we differ theologically and metaphysically, then we can discuss the attributes of Divinity calmly, clearly, and directly, without either blasphemy or unsupportable claims to the possession of certain knowledge.

Why should we not treat a theory about the Divine nature merely as a theory and then as theoreticians explore its consequences, along with its alternatives, without forming any special attachments? If we argue tenaciously on the practical level and seem certain of the basis for our knowledge there, why not theorize with equal ease on the abstract level also? In this way we can explore the following thesis: That our disagreements over the details of theology and metaphysics actually stem from our employment of fundamentally different concepts about the nature of the First Principle. Perhaps today we are once again ready to put first things first and to begin all philosophical theology and metaphysics, not with a theory of knowledge, but, as such clasical writers as Spinoza did, with the development of a theory about the Divine nature.

In any such construction as this, one of the first questions which must be dealt with is: What differentiates the Divine nature from any other nature? and the answer to this will always involve the formulation of a concept of perfection. For the Divine is divine only if it embodies qualities of perfection in a degree different from the human, or if it does so in a way fundamentally incapable of actualization within our natural order. Those who deny the existence of any First Principle, or of God, often do so because of an implicit rejection of the concept of a level or levels of existence higher and more perfect than that capable of realization within nature. Thus, the first task of the theologian is to make clear what it is for him that constitutes such unique qualities of perfection, i.e., what attributes serve to make the Divine divine and to set it apart forever from the natural order as prior because of its perfection.

The first part of this book simply attempts to set forth seven related theories about the nature of Divine perfection. The assumption is that disagreements on a fundamental metaphysical level can be shown to lie behind differences both in the conception of God and in questions about His actions toward men and the natural world. If we wish to come to understand God—or, perhaps more accurately, to understand the basis for our differences of opinion about the way in which God acts—we can do no better (so this brief book asserts) than to begin by attempting to sketch the various possible concepts of perfection. Having done this, we may then see more clearly the difficulties and the advantages which flow from the incorporation of one of these influential concepts into the construction of a systematic theory about God's attributes and actions.

How many in number are the possible concepts of Divine perfection? Such a question is unanswerable except to say that the history of both metaphysics and theology tells us that there is at least more than one and that, if we limit ourselves to only those types which differ from each other fundamentally, then the possible variations (and thus the possible sources of basic disagreement) are really rather few in number, and the alternatives are actually not quite so numerous as one might suppose. The future, of course, may disclose the formation of additional basic types of Divine perfection, but the potential reorganization and the fruitful exploration which would be made possible by such a discovery does not concern the present, except to lend excitement to the future.

One of the great virtues of exploring the question of Divine perfection is that it is at once a philosophical *and* a theological problem.

By no means is all of philosophy of interest to theologians or vice versa. Yet in a day in which philosophy and theology can and often do grow far apart, it is important to revive areas of equal interest to both disciplines. Of course, theology can hide under its skirts as many diverse pursuits as can philosophy, so that such a question as possible concepts of Divine perfection will tend to interest only the systematic theologians and the metaphysically inclined philosophers. However, such classical, constructive attempts are something which need encouragement in both fields. The question of the characteristics of Divine perfection has the happy advantage of uniting philosophers and theologians as equals in its exploration.

What does the notion of perfection as a metaphysical characteristic of the Divine nature have to do with the moral or religious use of the same term? Such an interrelating of similar moral or religious concepts is excluded from the scope of this inquiry, except to note that in recent generations much more attention has been paid to the ethical and to the religious than to the metaphysical. It just might be that the latter may prove to be the more fundamental. The aim of this book, then, is simply to set forth seven sets of theories of Divine perfection which seem to the writer to be both distinctive in kind and rich in consequence—rich metaphysically, theologically, and ethically. This will be done in Part I. In Part II six central pairs of metaphysical concepts will be considered which are crucial to the varying concepts of perfection.

This investigation will be at once historical and systematic. Philosophy and theology are no more and no less than what philosophers and theologians have written—which means that no philosopher or theologian can escape a study of the primary sources and still understand his discipline. In this sense no constructive work can ignore history. While the aim here is to set forth certain concepts of perfection which are systematically distinct, it would be a false attempt if it were not done through the medium of historical figures. Otherwise the systematic types, though interesting and possible, simply might not shed any light on what philosophy is or has been, but only on what it might be. On the other hand, a strong systematic interest prevents the types of Divine perfection outlined here from fitting the historical writings in every detail. The types of perfection presented will be generated out of historical material and applied to certain writers, but they will of necessity fit none of them with precise historical accuracy. The individual nature of philosophical and theological writing requires this slight distortion if the systematic purpose is to be accomplished. Such a blending and reworking of historical material is precisely the activity from which all creative metaphysics and theology derive their energy and their inspiration.

1

P L A T O

A N D

A R I S T O T L E

What is perfect is often said to mean what is complete or what has attained its end. Such a concept of perfection can easily be said to have dominated most of classical philosophy. Certainly this is true for both Plato and Aristotle. Plato's famous doctrine of the Forms has often been interpreted exclusively as an epistemological doctrine, which merely reflects the interest that has dominated modern thought. Actually, within the Platonic dialogues the Forms seem to be much more a standard of ontological perfection, giving simplicity and order to the world of sense and thus rendering it intelligible. The Forms serve as the model for the construction of the world in the *Timaeus*, to which the world-maker looks for his pattern.

For Aristotle form has an equally important place and similarly serves as a standard of perfection, although the concept of form is less universal and more closely embodied in the physical world, from which the individual mind abstracts it to gain knowledge. Form indicates completion, definiteness, limit, intelligibility, and exemption from motion. Aristotle's only deviation from Plato here is in the ontological status which he gives to form and in the conception of the process by which we come to know such an object. Essentially, however, both of these influential figures are united in their use of the properties of "form" to connote perfection.

Although form is the primary example of perfection for Plato, it is easy to see other characteristics of perfection at work in his dialogues. The guiding control of reason, the acquisition of knowledge of basic principles, the search for beauty, and the love or desire for increased knowledge—all of these are mentioned time after time. Transcendence is barely hinted at as a necessary aspect of perfection (notable exceptions: the description of the Good in the *Republic* and in the *Philebus*).

Virtue, of course, is one of Plato's main concerns, and this expresses itself theologically in the protest which appears in the first part of the *Republic* against the popular representations of the gods as indulging in human wickedness. Plato clearly links Divine perfection to moral virtue and in turn to stability of nature and lack of radical change in characteristics. Divinity requires unchangeableness of nature and a moral example of trustworthiness. Plato excludes motion as being an imperfection, though not as strongly as Aristotle does. The soul is the source of all motion; and in a way the soul also exemplifies perfection for Plato, although it does so in a secondary manner. On the whole, the eternal and changeless character of form stands as Plato's major criterion of perfection. It remains for Plotinus to pick up Plato's stress upon soul as an important ontological principle and then attempt to reconcile this with the motionless nature of perfection in a way in which Plato never did.

Control is another aspect of perfection which Plato stresses many times. Perhaps it is the major underlying theme of the *Republic*. The improvement of men and nations depends upon the union of abstract principles with practical power, with the philosopher-king standing as the symbol of rational control. The world-maker in the

Timaeus exemplifies this ideal control in a supreme sense, forcing into submission and to useful purpose the essentially chaotic elements in the receptacle. A world perfect in its self-maintainance is the end result of this kind of rational, controlled exercise of power.

Motion can never be completely excluded from the definition of perfection for Plato, since in the *Parmenides* the One which is beyond being is rejected as the dominant ontological principle. Instead, Plato settles for a continuous tension between absolute unity and sheer plurality. This yields the principle of definite number, and it indicates the ultimate, yet limited, pluralism inherent within Plato's ontological principles. Mixture thus becomes the guiding concept for perfection in the good life, as delineated in the *Philebus*. Guided by rationality and controlled by a preference for limitedness, mixture seems to be close to Plato's last word on the attributes of perfection. Either a world-maker or an individual man does the best he can with the material that is given to him without choice. He uses the power of rationality (guided through a knowledge of the interrelation of the Forms) to control, unify, and limit the ingredients in consonance with a concept of harmony and beauty.

Aristotle shows an even stronger preference for the limited and the complete as the very conditions for intelligibility and thus for perfection. Intelligibility and perfection both mean to be without matter, since matter entails division and motion, due to its incompleteness. To have completion means to have attained an end in harmony with the realization possible for that species. Development, motion, and seeking imply the lack of an attained end, and this characterizes what is as yet imperfect. In the *Metaphysics,* perfection in a being of the kind represented by the unmoved mover means not thinking about material (i.e., moving and thus imperfect) objects. Thought having its own completed thought as it object is the description of the unmoved mover's perfect state. Despite Aristotle's famed stress upon the centrality of the concrete individual in the process of knowledge, where ontological perfection is concerned his conception is on the whole quite abstract and free from motion.

It is in the concept of necessity that Aristotle differs perhaps most

fundamentally from Plato. To be such that it could not be otherwise, that is, to be necessary—this concept guides Aristotle in his
logical work and becomes crucial to his delineation of perfection.
Like Plato, he fully and freely recognizes the non-rational and the
accidental elements in all of nature. Like Plato also, however, he
looks not to all of nature for knowledge, but only to a part of it; and
this part Aristotle particularly stresses as the necessary, that which
alone is reducible to definite concept. Plato does not favor capricious-
ness in any sense, but his important principles of love and beauty
offer in their attractiveness to the mind a kind of counterpart to the
guidance Aristotle finds in that which cannot be other than it is,
i.e., the necessary in nature and in thought.

Aristotle's strongest words are reserved for the rejection of infinity or unlimitedness, since for him it means incompleteness, indeterminacy, and thus the impossibility of rational comprehension.
Aristotle limits his extended discussion only to the question of the
possibility of a material infinite, but it is no less clear that all kinds
of infinity are for him the antithesis of perfection. He admits fully
the importance and the difficulty of the question of whether or not
an actual infinite exists. He finally accepts the reality of a potential
infinite and of an actual infinity in the sense of perpetual circular
motion, since it has a limitation and a sense of continued completion.
Plato says little about the question of infinity, except to indicate his
possible receptiveness by including it as one of the basic principles
responsible for the origin of all things as he describes them in the
Philebus. In the *Sophist*, Plato does posit power as the fundamental
characteristic of all being, a principle which is not so hostile to
actual infinity. On the whole, however, Plato clearly agrees with
Aristotle in seeing limitation as reason's primary characteristic and
as the factor responsible for beauty, harmony, and thus, perfection.

Strangely enough, it is Aristotle, in the *Nicomachean Ethics*,
who stresses contemplation as being an activity that is akin to
divinity and as an end sufficient in itself. For all his supposed love of
abstract thought, Plato closely ties all perfect thought to a controlled
direction of the world's daily activities. Aristotle also stresses the

virtue of such practical wisdom, but that which is most god-like is that knowledge and contemplation which is sufficient in itself. The goal of thought seems to be such self-sufficiency as the unmoved mover has in his own self-reflective thought, and this concept is of major importance both for Aristotle's delineation of perfection and for many who come after him.

Like Plato, Aristotle rejects unity as a dominant feature of perfection. Since there is no radical distinction between perfection as it applies to ontological construction, to divinity, or to the rational part of man, unity in all three realms is reduced to merely the necessary element of order and limitation. Plato's Forms are plural, as are Aristotle's although those of both are limited in number. In the metaphysics of neither man can ontological first principles be reduced to one, or even ranked in strict order of importance according to any single and dominant concept. Limitation is important to both men, but Divine perfection retains an ultimately plural, if nevertheless definite, character.

One of the most influential concepts for all later thinking about Divine perfection is Aristotle's distinction between actual and potential and his unhesitating preference for the actual. This preference is easy to understand in light of the prevailing concepts of perfection, since potentiality involves change, time, motion, and incompleteness. It is hardly too much to say that Aristotle took the actual as his principal criterion for perfection, finding its epitome in the unmoved mover, whose very existence it is necessary to posit in order to find full actuality completely embodied. Later theologians agree overwhelmingly, and almost unconsciously, in making actuality one of the primary characteristics of Divine perfection. Potentiality comes to be ruled out of the Divine nature because of its opposition to actuality; and change, time, motion, and incompleteness are left to represent a lack of perfection. Although Plato does not use Aristotle's terms, he tends to share Aristotle's preference here without real difference.

Since motion is linked with time, change, and incompleteness, rest comes to be preferred and to represent perfection, not so much for its own sake but because it indicates a state of actuality. Eternity, as the absence of temporality, not mere indefinite extension of time, also shares this derived preference. Aristotle links time with motion, and motion with incompleteness, so that removal from direct participation in time becomes necessary to preserve pure actuality in any being that is to be called fully perfect. Thus, the specific terms in which Aristotle conceives perfection, and with which Plato does not essentially disagree, come to be linked firmly together and to define perfection for centuries to come.

2

PLOTINUS

AND THE

PSEUDO-DIONYSIUS

If Plato can be said to hint at times at the necessity for conceiving of the Divine as transcendent, it is safe to say that Aristotle does not see this necessity at all. It might be said that Aristotle rejects the existence of an actual infinite principally because of its quality of transcending intellection. He never speaks of the unmoved mover in a way that suggests anything other than an actual (i.e., pure) representation of the principles which are active within the natural order. Plato only suggests, but never develops, the concept of Good as transcending being and intellection. Aristotle cannot even go as far as a hint, but instead he rejects all transcendence and equates the ontologically perfect with what is amenable to full rational comprehension.

Although the Pre-Socratics are full of transcendental elements, it is really through the *Enneads* of Plotinus and the writings of the

Pseudo-Dionysius that western metaphysics and theology have come to think seriously of perfection's transcendence of being and reason. Such transcendence becomes not only compatible with, but even necessary to, any conception of Divine perfection. This comes about primarily through the emphasis given to unity as a central characteristic of anything worthy of being called perfect.

However, neither Plotinus nor Dionysius should be thought of as recommending the transcendence of being and of rationality as characteristic of perfection simply for the sake of transcendence. Especially in Plotinus, the element of transcendence of both the natural and the intelligible orders has its roots in Parmenides and in Plato's dialogue, *Parmenides*. In the latter, Plato considers the One beyond being and concludes that it is beyond all description and thought. Plotinus accepts this consequence in making the One his supreme First Principle, rather than follow Plato's more moderate (i.e., pluralistic) solution. When unity is made the supreme metaphysical concept, transcendence is a necessary consequence. Plato held to a compromise between unity and multiplicity (a dialectical tension), but Plotinus makes unity supreme and accepts the difficult consequences.

Yet, although transcendence comes to be attached to perfection because of the prominence of unity in governing ontological structure, the primacy of unity for Plotinus goes back another step. "Soul" was an important concept for Plato; to Plotinus it becomes all-important and philosophy's very starting point. To the very end, soul has an important but ambiguous role in Plato's dialogues. Plotinus begins with a systematic study of the soul and becomes the first classical philosopher to develop a subtle and profound psychology and to make such psychology central to philosophical thought. By comparison, Aristotle's treatise *On the Soul* is really only a theory of knowledge. Plotinus develops what can be called a metaphysic based upon an examination of soul, whereas Aristotle's metaphysics is surely based upon the principles of the physical world. Both Augustine and Hegel can be understood only against the backdrop of Plotinus' achievement.

In examining the soul and various extant theories about it, Plotinus concludes that soul is primarily characterized by a kind of organic unity. This degree of unity distinguishes the soul from lesser orders in the physical world and makes possible the development of a higher interior order within the soul. Despite its dispersal throughout the body, the soul has a degree of unity that prevents its becoming split as physical enties may be. The presence of the whole of the soul in each part simultaneously testifies to its non-material nature. Having distinguished the soul from physical nature and founded this distinction upon greater and lesser degrees of internal unity, Plotinus then discovers that the soul exists above the material world and is able to look either to it or away from it. Plotinus finds that when the soul is directed away from the physical world, it contemplates another sphere, the intelligible world. This realm proves to be above the soul because of its higher degree of unity. Pure thought does not look to the physical world, and thus such thought is not characterized by motion as is the soul. In fact, the intelligible world does not contain any possibility for division, except the necessary distinctions between thought and object, and between thought and thought.

Having transcended the physical and psychical world, guided by varying degrees of unity, the dialectical scale thus established naturally leads to its implied terminus, unity itself, absolutely without division. The actual description of the Plotinian First Principle is a complicated affair, but there is no question of the primacy assigned to unity as a metaphysical and theological concept or that it involves transcending both rationality and all of the natural characteristics of being. Here the law of identity is suspended, which is one reason that rationality is interrupted. All things are in the One as their source, but not as individual things. Here the negative method of approach becomes necessary, and all direct statement about the One becomes difficult, that is if normal standards of accuracy are expected to apply.

However, one difficulty in understanding Plotinus and one common source of misunderstanding about his doctrine is that nothing in his metaphysical hierarchy has only one side or aspect. Like

Spinoza, Plotinus holds that every important entity can be viewed in two ways, and different aspects will appear within each perspective. For Plotinus this duality of perspective is usually expressed in the metaphor "looking upward or looking downward." Each perspective is equally true, although of course the way up, i.e., toward increasing unity and the One itself, is the primary route, just as for Spinoza "under the aspect of eternity" provides the more adequate understanding. But this duality of perspective often leads to apparently conflicting statements, and it always leads to complexity and intricacy of metaphysical structure.

All of this helps us to understand why Plotinus says a great deal about his ultimate principle, the One, and at the same time gives good reasons why description of it and direct statement about it are both impossible and misleading when attempted. The underlying principle of unity, uncovered through his analysis of the status of the soul, forces Plotinus to maintain the extreme transcendence of what is ultimately perfect; but duality of perspective (represented in the negative method of approach) still allows him to give a full discussion of the supremely perfect One. All that is found within the structure of being, even Plotinus' Intellectual Principle (akin to Plato's Forms), involves some degree of duality, which forces the supremely perfect One to stand beyond intellection and outside both the structure of being and of not-being. Unity as the supreme (and, of course, singular) characteristic of what is ultimately perfect will now involve Divine perfection in the difficulties and the protective advantages of the extreme transcendence of rational structure.

Sometimes Plotinus calls his First Principle the Good, indicating its freely creative and outgoing tendency. When so characterized, the supremely perfect becomes abundantly full and is viewed as the source of all structures and of all beings within the natural world. However, it seems clear that the principle of identity is derivative from the One and not applicable to it. Thus, when the One is described as containing all things while yet itself being nothing, it is precisely because the suspension of the normal, so-called "laws of thought" results in a unique situation within the One. It cannot be described by means of our normal distinctions; within it all is present but without limit, distinction, or precise boundary.

Divine, or really more properly, ultimate perfection (since "divine" as we use it applies in Plotinus' hierarchy to the secondary realm of intelligence), although perhaps not beyond all grasp, is dominated not by a group of characteristic perfections but by a single, dominant one. Personality is surpassed, just as intellection was, and all contingency or variability in the world's creation and constitution is ruled out. What is supremely perfect is neither limited nor unlimited, finite nor infinite, but transcends these and all other such oppositions and distinctions. It is both supremely actual and supremely potential, since it contains all things as their ultimate source, but it does so in a manner beyond normal distinctions. This means that the One cannot be called actual as opposed to potential, but must be both without being either separately.

Such breaking of normal thought categories, already strained where Divine perfection is concerned, makes perfection hard to characterize in any satisfactory manner. One certain characteristic remains, however: self-sufficiency. What is supremely perfect now cannot be described by any simple set of characteristics such as rest vs. motion. Yet never is any First Principle made dependent on anything other than itself (once the era of a single First Principle is reached). In fact, the transcendence of categories and distinctions by the Plotinian One seems to be propelled by the very desire to place what is to be adjudged ultimately perfect as forever beyond all dependence, the dependence which any structure or list of distinct characteristics must involve.

Although neither necessity nor freedom is quite accurate as an exclusive characteristic of perfection for Plotinus, necessity (as for Aristotle) is more important if it is contrasted with the possible, i.e., with the world we now have as it is conceived in alternative forms. Choice involves distinctions and is not characteristic of the One. The One produces ungrudgingly and without omission or lack, but it is not a contemplated production or an act which involves any alternatives. Eternity is not quite properly applicable to the One,

except insofar as it is different from the temporal in being its source. Nor is infinity characteristic of the One, since that involves multiplicity. The One is beyond both the finite and the infinite as the undivided source of both.

However, good does apply to the One; in fact Plotinus often uses the Good as a synonym for the One. The Good is the One regarded in its relation to the Intellectual Principle which it produces. Regarded as the source of all levels of being, the One is good and is the opposite of all evil. Evil comes to be measured in distance from the One, taken in its capacity as the source of all. Power certainly is basic to such a conception of the One as the origin of all things, although descriptions of the One itself tend to produce a feeling of quietude and calm. Once again, what is important in the metaphysical structure of the One is that it allows two apparently opposed descriptions. On the other hand, the One's perfection certainly places it ultimately above even a dual mode of knowledge. Knowing violates unity by being dependent upon the distinctions it is necessary to make between thought and its object.

Like self-sufficiency, the One is cause-of-itself as opposed to cause-in-another, although even this distinction is not wholly adequate as applied to the One. As to being vs. non-being, it transcends both as the source of both, which of course means that the perfection of the One is not that of being as opposed to non-being. All of this sublety of hierarchy and difficulty of attribution leads Plotinus to a definite preference for the negative method of approach. Direct and positive statements, even when balanced by negative ones, seem to require a containment of the One within the basic structures of being, and the stress on unity as primal in perfection makes the transcendence of being and intellection absolutely necessary. The complexities and the difficulties which this introduces into any description of Divine (or supra-Divine) perfection are, and were, far reaching.

The Pseudo-Dionysius can be viewed within the Plotinian framework of perfection with little modification or distortion. Perfection as requiring transcendence of being and intellection is reflected on every page. Dionysius asserts his preference for the negative method,

and mysticism of a disciplined sort is necessary because of the distortion of perfection which remains in even the most refined thought, since thought cannot exist without distinctions. With an interest in Christian categories, Dionysius leaves room for a trinitarian concept and an attribution of personality to his Supreme. However, the ultimate way in which these distinctions are present within the First Principle cannot be made precise. Plotinus, too, can locate all within the One if it is viewed as the source of all distinctions, and Dionysius locates Christian attributes in his First Principle in much the same way.

Dionysius' treatise *On the Divine Names* indicates the necessity for Christians to speak directly about God. The action of God in an historical event and the existence of a sacred literature which speaks casually and often of God, these make Dionysius more interested in considering carefully the applicability of a series of names to God. As every skilled theologian must, Dionysius totally rejects some names as unworthy, others as partially so, and still others he finds to be even more appropriate (i.e., undifferenced names, applicable without distinction to the whole of the Godhead). However, here symbolism develops as an explicit method in a way that was not required by Plotinus' metaphysical problems.

The result is that some names may be applied to the Divine perfection, but these are neither ultimate nor ultimately distinct. Rather, such appropriate names direct us; they stand as symbols and signs for what finally transcends both name and description. Theological language becomes necessarily non-literal and symbolic whenever Divine perfection is conceived primarily in terms of a unity that demands the abrogation of distinctions. A search for appropriate Divine names ends by taking the seeker beyond all names and distinctions. As in Plotinus, describing Divine perfection leads you not only beyond this world but beyond intellection and direct speech.

Theology since Plotinus and Dionysius has continually faced the problem of the transcendence of perfection beyond the confines of both being and language. Yet both Plotinus and Dionysius are often misunderstood and thought to be saying that nothing at all can be

said about such a transcendent First Principle. As a matter of fact, both devote great energy to describing their Supreme Principle. Dionysius keeps his Super-essential Godhead somewhat closer to usual conceptions of divinity, but our ordinary language nevertheless becomes both inadequate and symbolic. Plotinus' One cannot even be called "God" in any usual sense. The normal characteristics of a Divinity are more to be found in the lower levels, although all levels are also in the One without distinction as in their source.

Rational discourse, Divine as it is, is now seen as involving the imperfection of some distinction, however minor it may be. And distinction is to be avoided because it may permit division, which would impair Divine self-sufficiency, the most prized perfection. Being is no longer a supreme concept, nor is non-being, since the primary consequence of this view of perfection is that the law of identity holds only for the realms below the First. Negation, and the creation of new terms to serve as symbols, is characteristic of this approach. Final statements are ruled out by the ultimate inappropriateness of a language that is necessarily based upon distinctions. Unity, the primary Divine perfection, has powerful transforming and attractive qualities; but it also creates subtle and difficult problems wherever clear and accurate statement is attempted. Such perfection certainly makes it hard to degrade a First Principle, but it also renders precise statement necessarily improbable.

Dionysius is even forced to place his Supreme God beyond perfection, a not uncommon ending for a neo-Platonist. This, of course, does not mean that God is imperfect but simply indicates that his transcendence of normal categories is such that our usual conceptions of perfection (e.g., Aristotle's definition in terms of what is limited and complete) are too confining. He is beyond standard concepts of perfection and imperfection as the source of both. The source of standards must be greater than the limits of the standards and must go beyond their immediate confines.

3

AUGUSTINE

AND

ANSELM

Perhaps no figure in the history of philosophy and theology is more difficult or more important to understand than Augustine. His writings are voluminous, but they hold to no recognized systematic form, neither that of brevity, consciously imposed structure, nor complete consistency of viewpoint. It is no exaggeration to say that Augustine began by endorsing pagan Roman philosophy and only gradually began to remold this as he pondered over the problems of Christian doctrine. He has an affinity with the Platonic and neo-Platonic tradition in both his early use of dialogue and the looseness of his technical terms and his doctrine. Yet no figure looms so large in influencing later theological thinking on Divine perfection.

Except perhaps in the work *On the Trinity,* Augustine never treats the metaphysical problem of the perfection of Divinity in a straightforward manner, yet it is fairly easy to see his views on perfection reflected with amazing consistency in all of his writing. God is first and foremost characterized by immutability, and this central quality of His perfection guides Augustine to many a doctrinal decision. More akin to Plato and Aristotle on this point than to Plotinus, Augustine views any form of change as evidence of imperfection, and the strength of this conviction has much to do with his important doctrine of Divine foreknowledge and predestination.

Other than immutability, God's primary perfection seems to be wisdom. Here we can see even more clearly that, especially in his conception of God, Augustine did not follow Plotinus as he is often supposed to have done. Unity is stressed as a characteristic of Divinity but an ultimate trinity is allowed, and wisdom as the central characteristic of Divine perfection indicates the essential reasonableness and lack of extreme transcendence which Augustine finds in the Divine nature. Wisdom, the supreme source of all knowledge, and immortality reduce unity to a lesser perfection.

Perhaps in his doctrine of the soul Augustine can be seen to be most like Plotinus, even if this similarity is not to be found in his ultimate metaphysical structure. Augustine's psychology is detailed and profound. As in Plotinus, an analysis of the soul often serves as a systematic point of departure; and, in the case of both the Trinity and time, it is within the soul that analysis discloses structures which can serve as the basis for rendering intelligible both time and the trinitarian nature of God. Our psychology reveals a certain distinction present within the unity of our mind (e.g., memory, intellect, and will, operating together), and these insights into our own nature give us a genuine basis for understanding God.

It is no easy task to understand Augustine's attempt to assure Divine foreknowledge of all events and actions, without either asserting God to be the immediate cause or impairing freedom of action. However, as far as Divine perfection is concerned, the important point is that it is Augustine's desire to prevent any change in God or in His knowledge which makes Augustine hold so forcefully to the doctrine of absolute foreknowledge and also the eternality of God. The situation is similar for the doctrine of evil. Since God created even eternity and knows all things from eternity and is primarily characterized by rest, evil comes to be thought of as a lesser good, defined by its closeness or distance from the Divine nature. All actions are immediately present to God's knowledge, so that evil is robbed of any independent status by its immediate and eternal presence in God and must be accounted for as a part of what is essentially a completely good nature.

Augustine speaks little about such technical attributes of perfection as infinity, although he appears to ascribe it to God in a positive, if not in an important, sense. God is certainly rational, determinate, complete, and actual in His perfection, although Augustine is not often given to arguing such questions explicitly. Rest is certainly a primary characteristic, both religiously and metaphysically. Real alternatives to the structure of this world do not seem either important or possible to Augustine. God's nature is mirrored fully in this world, especially in men's minds.

The famous doctrine of time is perhaps most important here, along with the trinitarian aspects that Augustine finds rooted in our own psychology. Elaborating Plato's brief characterization of time as "the moving image of eternity," Augustine finds memory and expectation (i.e., past and future) to exist only as they are held together in the present. Our time moves; God holds all parts of time present in simultaneous and changeless vision. God, then, is actually not extremely unlike men in His Divinely perfect nature. He escapes the disintegrating tendencies of time and place. He creates time but is not Himself in time. He is a trinity as we are a trinity of memory, understanding, and will; but He is at rest and is above us as the creator of all things, although it is through our minds that we may be intimately and immediately made aware of God. God does not transcend wisdom because of His perfection; He is wisdom par excellence—creative, immutable, and at rest.

This lack of the transcendence which perfection has often demanded leads Augustine to prefer the direct and simple attribution of characteristics to God, rather than the more torturous and tenuous *via negativa*. So close does he see the analogy of God to the human mind and soul that Augustine experiences no great difficulty in speaking about God in a straightforward and simple manner. His supreme wisdom, His moral perfection, and His omnipotence as creator of the world and man make God forever different from man. Although all words are signs or symbols for Augustine and not literal knowledge, speaking about God poses no insurmountable difficulties imposed by His perfection.

Anselm, like Augustine, must be read with the general Platonic framework in mind, and much misunderstanding has resulted from not doing so. It is true that he is a more systematic writer than Augustine, but beneath his dialectic can be seen again a looseness of basic structure and, what is more important, a certain detachment and tentativeness about all of the reasonings he puts forth. As for Augustine, so for Anselm thought about God takes the form of an attempt to arrive at an adequate concept. Despite the popular conception of his method, Anselm does not begin with a finished concept. All discussion is an exercise for the mind and all statement a testing ground for the mind, enabling it to check the adequacy of its concepts by comparison. A non-dogmatic flavor is ever present in Anselm, and his doctrine of God especially should be taken as a starting point, not a conclusion, intended by him to be suggestive to the inquiring mind.

Immutability again seems to be central in considering Divine perfection, and all reasoning takes the form of trying to rid the attributes we assign to God of any imperfect connotations. As in Augustine, degrees of value play an important role in increasing the mind's knowledge of God. In fact, the whole of the discussion in both the *Monologium* and the *Proslogium* is an effort to make the mind rise to an apprehension of God through considering what attribute is more perfect than another and what is absolutely perfect. We begin with certain traditional notions of God's perfection and then raise the mind above its normal field of vision by attempting to strip God's usual attributes of any aspects which would place Him beneath anything else. We begin with the most perfect conception we can form and, through questioning it, improve our grasp of what Divine perfection really means.

Perhaps the most important notion which emerges from the changes which take place in Anselm's early and too easy formulations of the ontological argument is that God is not simply the highest being the mind can conceive but *transcends conception.* Thus Anselm introduces a transcendental element into perfection that is not so strongly present in Augustine or even present at the beginning of his own formulation. However, Anselm introduces a subtle distinction into his discovery that God's perfection requires an ultimately ineffable nature by asserting that, although our terms refer to a being beyond comprehension, the meanings of the terms used in describing God are in themselves fully comprehensible. Thus, God is no idea in the mind of any man, not even the idea of the most perfect being, although our consideration of this preliminary concept of perfection can lead us to form more adequate concepts and eventually to see the necessarily limited accuracy of all conception and naming.

Anselm's characterization of God takes the very traditional form of listing the important names ascribed to God and then considering the adequacy of some of them. His fundamental belief in the non-temporality of God governs much of his qualification of the traditional attributes. God's immutability must not be jeopardized by any predication which makes God in any way relative. Perfection demands that God exist solely in and through Himself. All attempted attribution merely serves the function of leading us to see the independence of God from all normal structures of being. We predicate perfections of Him, e.g., goodness, only as a means of raising our own minds. We say this not in order to conceive of Him as possessing that quality, or any other, but to discover Him as being goodness itself and as bestowing that quality and all other perfections on this created world.

Although Anselm gives in fairly rapid order a traditional list of the Divine attributes, which properly conceived constitute Divine perfection, he does not discuss many of them in detail. The perfections which are to be attributed to God seem at this point in theological history to be fairly well established, and the problem is to order and to give structure to them. Anselm does focus on God's non-temporality, which places him well within the more traditional conceptions of Divine perfection. Goodness is an attribute Anselm also stresses in the *Monologium,* which allies him with Augustine in seeing God's perfection as the supreme source of all the degrees and kinds of goodness embodied in the orders of this world.

The force of Anselm's ontological argument, since it depends upon God's absolute uniqueness as a rational object, results in God's transcendence of normal conception and rational grasp. This is based upon the now standard characterization of God's perfection: infinite, non-temporal, self-existent, and possessing all power. It does not involve the extreme transcendence of the neo-Platonic variety, since unity, though included, is not the dominant attribute of Divine perfection. Negative theology is not Anselm's mode of approach; God's perfection is not so extreme as to demand it. Anselm's approach is direct and straightforward. However, after a brief encounter with the traditional attributes, God is found to transcend any preliminary idea we may have formed. Anselm maintains that if we begin by thinking of Him as highest in the known scale of things (e.g., "that than which nothing greater can be conceived"), further reflection on the perfection of such a being reveals Him to be greater than any normal conception and thus beyond conception, not merely at its limit.

If the *Proslogium* and *Appendix* make the "proof" for God's existence depend (1) upon His transcendence of normal conceptualization and (2) upon the admission of the argument's uniqueness which is due to the special nature of the object, then the *Monologium* can be seen as a "meditation" on the characteristics of God which are such that they require a transformation of all thought which is to be about Him. Anselm begins with the traditional valuational approach, making God alone supremely good, He who is alone good through Himself. Since all things are not embraced in a single degree of dignity, the contrast of levels of existence leads us to conceive of God's nature as deriving existence from itself. Thus, "self-existent cause" and "supremely good through itself" become the two chief characteristics of Divine perfection, and they cause God to be set over against all other natures as radically different in kind from them.

Creating through expressing His eternal ideas, creating by taking absolutely nothing from any other source—these are the next most important perfections which Anselm finds in God. In any Christian conception, God's perfection demands that His creative power be unobstructed and be dependent upon nothing outside of Him. God need not, as is sometimes thought, create from or depend upon absolutely nothing; He simply depends upon *nothing outside* Himself. Such a creative source can be described as "living," which under other circumstances might be considered a second-order perfection. Compositeness within the Divine nature must still be denied; thus, after listing the Divine attributes, the problem is to demonstrate the ultimate unity of them all. The reconciliation of the multiple statements which must be made about God is a task which unity as a central perfection demands of all theologians and metaphysicians.

4

AQUINAS

AND

OCKHAM

In the writings of Thomas Aquinas and William of Ockham, and in John Duns Scotus too, definite changes begin to be revealed in the way in which Divine perfection is conceived. In Aquinas, such changes are contained within a traditional framework, but in the writings of either Scotus or Ockham these changes can be seen to have broken through to the surface and to have produced alterations in the basic metaphysical principles of both of these writers.

Despite the renowned difficulties of language and thought structure that characterize the writings of Scotus and Ockham, in some respects their basic positions are easier to grasp than is that of Thomas. Taking the two *Summas* of Thomas as an example, we find between those covers an enormous collection of views, derived from the famous model of the medievals' basic text, the *Sentences*. Without attempting here to analyse the complex structure and style of the *Summas,* the real difficulty for their clear interpretation stems from the wide variety of views which Thomas brings together in those pages. It is a complex job to see Thomas' position clearly on any issue, and he is often done the great disservice of oversimplification, or what is worse of oversystematization, and this leads to stereotyped doctrines and rigidified views. Augustine and the neo-Platonic Pseudo-Dionysius are quoted by Thomas frequently and at crucial points, so that any attempt to overstress Aristotle's influence is deceptive. The key to understanding Aquinas lies in the reconciliation of the almost wild variety of sources upon which he draws, a fascinating and baffling undertaking.

Perhaps nowhere is the contrast between Thomas and Aristotle more clearly seen than in Aquinas' doctrine of the Divine nature. The unmoved mover is never really discussed at length by Aristotle, and hardly at all outside the *Metaphysics* or *Physics,* whereas God is the center of and plays the largest part in Aquinas' thought. Aristotelian terminology, it is true, is often used in the *Summas,* but this similarity can be misleading. Where God is concerned, Aquinas is much closer to the Platonists and the neo-Platonists (mediated via Augustine), the Pseudo-Dionysius and the many other followers of this tradition whom he so often quotes.

One example is particularly illuminating in this connection: the relation of "infinity" and "form." In the *Physics* especially, Aristotle goes to great pains to deny the existence of an actual (corporeal) infinite. Admitting that the problem will remain puzzling under any solution, Aristotle accepts the existence of an infinite in the sense of potentiality (e.g., the potential division *ad infinitum* of any corporeal body) and perhaps also in uninterrupted and eternal circular motion. However, even this limited admission of the infinite does not remove its incompatibility with form (since form necessitates limit) or remove its opposition to both reason and perfection. Reason depends upon form, which requires limitation, and perfection requires completion and pure actuality, the opposite of the infinite as potential.

Aquinas deals with the problem by denying the incompatibility of infinity with form and removing the general question from the context of a *corporeal* infinite, changing the question to one of infinity in the *incorporeal* Divine nature. Thomas agrees with Aristotle where the corporeal infinite is concerned, but he then goes on to apply infinity as a perfection to God alone, having reversed Aristotle and made the infinite compatible with form and actuality. The acceptance of infinity as a perfection within the Divine nature requires a change in the Aristotelian metaphysics which could hardly be more fundamental. It is true that the importance of form is maintained, as it is not in some other conceptions of perfection, and it is also true that the perfection of the Divine nature does not require the transcendence of being. However, both limitation and the necessary connection by Aristotle of infinity with incompleteness are reversed by Thomas. It could not even have occurred to Aristotle to consider infinity as a perfection or to raise the question in connection with the nature of his unmoved mover; now infinity has become the very hallmark of perfection for theologians considering the Divine nature.

It is the unforgettable legacy of neo-Platonism that causes Aquinas to begin his systematic consideration of the Divine attributes with the affirmation of the simplicity of God. Religiously speaking, of course, this has its roots also in the traditional Hebrew affirmation, "Hear, O Israel, the Lord Our God is One God"; but, technically speaking, it is Plotinus and his kin who have impressed upon us all the primacy of simplicity wherever ontological perfection is concerned. This is all the more important for Thomas, since his basically non-transcendent (i.e., not beyond being) view of God's perfection causes him to attribute many characteristics to God, including a trinitarian nature and the essential characteristics of personality, so that the maintenance of simplicity is a difficult and a pressing question.

Thomas begins his consideration of the Divine nature with a variation on the traditional negative method, by denying of Him whatever is opposed to the idea of Him, e.g., "it is absolutely true that God is not a body" (Pt. 1, p3, Art. 1). Following this comes Thomas' major item of agreement with Aristotle, the assertion of the absolute priority of actuality (i.e., no motion, change, or unrealized aspect) which dominates most of the theological tradition and safeguards the Divine self-sufficiency and omnipotence. Matter is of course denied as applicable to God, due to its linkage with potentiality; and God's existence is identical with His essence, since otherwise He would be among those things whose existence is caused by something outside of themselves. However, God is not to be found in any genus. He transcends ordinary classification but He does not transcend being itself, nor is He a subject of whom accidents may be predicated. He rules all things without commingling with them.

Perfection is literally equated by Thomas with degree of actuality. He follows Aristotle here, but he departs from him later to make existence the most perfect of all things. All created perfections preexist in God in a more eminent manner, since He is the world's cause in a way in which Aristotle's unmoved mover could never be. Thus, things diverse and in themselves opposed to each other preexist in God as one, without injury to His simplicity. It is quite significant that, in making this unusual reconciliation of multiplicity with unity, Thomas quotes Dionysius no fewer than five times. Goodness is equated with being, and God's immutability is deduced as a consequence of His infinity and His pure actuality. He is eternal, apprehending all things as simultaneously whole and without motion. God's unity consists of His indivisibility, His most jealously guarded attribute in traditional thought.

Since one of Aristotle's primary reasons for rejecting an actual infinite was its unknowability (since comprehension depends upon limitation), Thomas' admission of an actual infinite in the single case of the Divine nature poses a problem of knowledge. Since infinity cannot be directly comprehended, Thomas must make the ultimate vision of God a matter of Divine grace, which is the raising of the natural intellect to a higher mode of knowledge. God does not transcend being, but, since He is infinite form, He transcends all ordinary modes of knowledge. Since Aquinas agrees with Aristotle on the necessity of limitation in natural knowledge, no natural knowledge of the Divine nature itself is attainable. It is possible to see the essence of God, but not by means of natural knowledge.

In this view, faith becomes a kind of knowledge. And in the end, Thomas seems to follow the transcendentalists and to deny that multiplicity in the Divine nature is constitutive of His nature. Multiplicity is due solely to the fact that the weakness of our intellect forces us to apprehend Him in a manifold manner. Distinctions and multiplicity are finally seen to have only an epistemological basis— i.e., they are derived solely from the limitations of our mode of knowledge and are not applicable to God as He is in Himself. At the crucial moment of the apprehension of the Divine nature, Plotinus triumphs and Aristotle fails.

The revolution which Thomas pioneered, and which led to an eventual transformation, results from the ascriptions of an infinity of possibles to the Divine intellect. With infinity elevated to a perfection, it is unthinkable to limit God's knowledge to the finite entities of this world. Thus, there are other things in God's knowledge, and also in His power, than the actual beings of this world. Although the possibles are not—nor will be, nor were—in existence, still, they are known by God and exist as possibles in the Divine intellect. Thomas even goes so far as to say that a better world than this was and is in God's power. However, since Thomas never gives up the priority of actuality or the subservience of the Divine will to both goodness and the Divine nature as a whole, no other world than this is genuinely possible other than in conception. Contingency in the Divine activity would be incompatible with a perfection that is defined primarily by actuality. In the doctrine of the possibles present in the infinity of the Divine knowledge, Aquinas has the seeds for a revolution in the concept of perfection, though not its accomplishment.

Aquinas allows for an actual infinite, but in God alone and only in the infinity of form. Nevertheless, this removes the traditional Aristotelian linkage of form and being with limitedness. This compatibility of form with infinity removes the usual classical objection to infinity as indeterminate and incomplete and leaves infinity free to become a perfection. Form implies actuality, so that any infinite, if it is compatible with form, is subject to none of the usual objections of involvement with potentiality and motion. Although such infinity of form allows the presence of unactualized possibles in the Divine intellect, yet the lack of real freedom in God's choice in creation prevents this unrealized realm from involving God in any serious potentiality. He remains above time, since the exact plan of actualization in the act of creation is determined from eternity.

God's goodness here plays a major role, specifying which possibles necessarily comprise the set to be actualized, and this eliminates any indeterminacy in God's nature or in His action. What God has present in His intellect are universal concepts, through which individuals are known as parts, but this mode of knowing effectively prevents any direct involvement of the Divine nature with the difficulties of particularity. Such a God is transcendent only as involving infinity vs. finiteness, and, as regards his full actuality, not as existing beyond being or knowable form. Thus, His simplicity and unity are not for Thomas of the extreme kind of a Dionysius or Plotinus. However, there are times, as I have indicated, when Thomas seems to take it all back and to make all distinctions seen in God only a reflection of the inadequacies of our mode of knowledge rather than a sign of any real distinction present within and constitutive of the Divine nature.

Thomas advocates the negative method, but it seems to be mainly a method of approach which human beings find necessary, not actually indicative of any transcendence of reason required by the Divine nature itself. Positive and directly applicable attributes result from the negative method, and the method proceeds by denying predication according to an already present conception of God. In line with such a view, it is particularly significant to note Thomas' conclusion that the eternality of the world cannot be disproved reasonably and that creation *ex nihilo* has to be held as an article of faith. This is perfectly consistent with the general classical framework within which Aquinas sets the embryonic form of a few transforming concepts. Novel elements are present, but the overall scheme is still classically rational and eternal and necessary.

Using Ockham as an example of the more radical ontology which arises both in his writings and in those of Duns Scotus, a new ontological framework begins to appear, and as a consequence Divine perfection undergoes a major transformation. Perhaps most significant is Ockham's explicit announcement that his aim is to rid theology of the Greek-derived divine, immutable, and universal forms. His famed nominalism thus must really be understood theologically and, furthermore, as aimed specifically at opening up the Divine nature to the freedom of alternative action. Ockham saw the traditional universal ideas in the mind of God as binding God to necessary action, both in knowing and in creating. The removal of these universal ideas and the substitution of an absolute infinity of possible *individuals* is the systematic basis for the famous dictum: All things are possible for God, save such as involve a contradiction.

In understanding Ockham's fundamental revisions in the conception of Divine perfection, it is almost more important to read his writing and to feel the novel cast of his approach than it is to know a few formal doctrines. There is a certain air of detachment, characteristic of the logical temperament, and especially a sense of the equal possibility of several arguments or modes of approach. Any proposition seems entertainable here, with relative merit and weight assigned by careful consideration. Much of his terminology, and certainly his style of composition, evidence the classical rigor of the logician. Some of the modern temperament is here, but, most important, there is not the modern abandonment of classical problems. All traditional issues appear, but in a new guise.

Truth and possibility are most rigorously defined. There is scientific knowledge only of what remains true regardless of the existence or non-existence of our world, which renders all statements about our world contingent. Possibility is limited not by the structure of our world but merely by the demands of logic for the absence of internal contradiction. Thus, our mind is immediately directed away from the specifics of the structure which we happen to know toward a logical structure of infinite extent, of which our order involves only a small part and but a few of the rules. The possible approaches to God are increased, but the finality of any statement is also proportionally reduced. We now deal in possibles and in possible statements, not in necessities and necessary conclusions.

Most important for our knowledge of the Divine nature is the statement that we cannot have a concept of God that is both simple and at the same time proper to God. Here it is important to remember that, for Ockham, we are always dealing with constructed logical concepts *about* God, never *with* God Himself. Thus, our position requires us to construct a concept of God out of various pieces, which means that the result must necessarily reflect the complexity of our approach. We may most certainly reason about God with probability, but never with certainty. It follows that we *cannot demonstrate* that there is only one God, although we can give complex reasons for the *preferability* of a single First Principle.

Ockham gives variety in philosophy a systematic basis: he maintains that one may safely hold different and opposite opinions regarding the mind of any author, if he is not the author of Holy Scriptures. Such variety is not injurious either to God or to religion, since a real science is not about things but about mental contents standing for things. Our mental contents do stand for things, but as they are not the things themselves, philosophical thought is free to follow a variety of modes of analysis of all possible mental contents. This detachment has its most startling result in the famous assertion that God could cause in us the immediate intuition of a non-existent sense object. To a world not so totally absorbed in epistemology as ours, this is not too devastating a possibility, since it arises and is considered merely as a logical possibility, with no particular attention at the moment to its actual likelihood in fact.

This is a view of Divine perfection which stresses its unlimited aspect, limiting possibility only by the necessity of non-contradiction, but keeping perfection within rational bounds by that single qualification. For "being" is defined by infinite possibles, themselves limited only by the necessity of containing no internal contradiction.

But this restriction prevents the unlimited aspect of being from becoming indefinite, the quality which had previously often raised infinity above being and beyond rationality. Being as it applies to God is limited only by possibility, but rationality and will (as coordinate Divine attributes) keep this from involving God in indeterminateness. However, God is not fully actual, as traditional doctrines require, in the sense that His will and power have not actualized all of the infinite and individual possibles that His intellect comprehends.

Divine perfection has been fundamentally altered, but the central characteristic which all sought to preserve remains, i.e., self-sufficiency. The existence of unrealized possibles within the Divine nature seemed to earlier writers to involve God's nature in the indefinite and the indeterminate and thus to jeopardize the Divine self-sufficiency. Ockham, however, conceives possibility as unlimited but rational, so that when possibility is linked with the Divine will and understanding, it is able to preserve the necessary quality of the Divine as contrasted with the human, i.e., self-sufficiency. But does this involve the Divine nature in motion, change, and time? No, since God's power is unrestricted (except by the prohibition of self-contradiction), and His intellect is actually applicable to the full range of possibles simultaneously.

What is crucial, however, is that while God is not necessarily involved in motion, change, and time, His action does become free, i.e., contingent. This both Ockham and Scotus wished to achieve, freeing the Divine action from necessity and thus opening human action to the same possibility that God is conceived to possess. God's power remains infinite and His omnipotence is unquestioned, but His action in creation is contingent on the final decision of His will, subject only to the requirements of rationality and the limitations imposed by the conditions necessary to constitute a creation. Criteria of good and evil are operative here, but not in such a way as to necessitate the actualization of only one set from among the possible individuals. It is Duns Scotus who sees most clearly that the Divine nature must be so conceived as to make its action in some sense contingent before there can be any hope of finding freedom (i.e., contingency) in man's action.

Ockham's view retains another essential quality of Divinity: cause-of-itself—and all created things continue to locate the cause of their existence in another being. A doctrine of creation is necessary, because there is now the need for a power sufficient to actualize the finite set of possibles which constitute our world, as contrasted with the infinite set of possible individuals. Within the Divine nature and compatible with its perfection non-being exists as the presence of logically consistent but unrealized possible individuals—the Divine will and power did not attach to their primitive ancestors. And the Divine nature, i.e., our constructed conception of it, becomes necessarily complex, although unity is sustained through the unity of the action of the Divine will and power, working under the conditions of rational conception. Positive attribution is possible where the Divine nature is concerned; this view of perfection does not require the negative approach. Essentially univocal predication may be made concerning God, although the procedure is intricate and highly structured.

5

MEISTER ECKHART

AND

NICOLAS CUSANUS

The recent widespread interest in Thomas Aquinas has often served to distort the picture of the philosophical and theological thought of his time, primarily by oversimplifying its complexity. Certain simplified theories of historical development have also obscured the fact that during the entire Middle Ages philosophical thought continually exhibited wide variety. The mystical and the neo-Platonic strains particularly are often underestimated as to their strength and their continued influence. Recent thought, both in philosophy and theology, has not been very sympathetic to the late medieval tradition, and yet without it such a contemporary theologian as Tillich and such influential philosophers as Hegel are not understandable. It is true that one can find in Plotinus and Dionysius a classical locus for all later transcendental tendencies, but in

Eckhart and Cusanus certain novel developments appear which make them decisively modern.

Eckhart is clear in following traditional neo-Platonism: There are no distinctions in God, the Divine nature is One. Although the trinitarian doctrine is added, it is construed so as to make each person of the trinity the same One in nature. Although such stress upon unity and the lack of distinction is quite classical, in Eckhart's doctrine of "disinterest" novel elements appear. Plotinus uses good and beauty as primary ways to speak about the One, but Eckhart puts disinterest higher than love. In retrospect, it appears that the extreme quietude and emptiness, so often thought of in connection with the perfection of the Plotinian One, are actually a development of a much more modern strain of thought. "Emptiness" is not a term Plotinus could possibly use about a fecund One, although the One does stand above distinction and above knowing. In Eckhart unity is made to follow from the Divine's primary quality, disinterest. Both love and unity are in God, but they are secondary and follow from the higher quietude of disinterest.

In Plotinian thought the One is reached through increasing fullness; for Eckhart the cultivation of disinterest in the individual alone brings God to him. The Plotinian ascent is somewhat reversed, and we see the new humanism at work. When a mind is really freed through disinterest, God is compelled to come. The center of attention is the human psychological state, and here one is reminded of the writings of Kierkegaard. Disinterest is the Divine perfection; it gives God his status as God; disinterest brings man into his closest resemblance to God. And thus stated, disinterest as the highest Divine perfection does not remove man by structure far from God, since by spiritual discipline man can achieve disinterest and thus likeness to the Divine nature. To be empty of things is to be full of God. The Plotinian One is full of all things as their source and is no one thing in distinction, but the idea of emptiness is foreign to Plotinus and central for Eckhart.

Pure disinterest is empty nothingness. Such a description of God's highest perfection has no classical counterpart. It entails a lack of action, and the soul of man is also seen to lack action at its center. God has no ideas nor does He need any. The soul is the arena of His activity, and His action there is without instrument. Here we have the source of the concepts of "wilderness" and of "alienation" from self and from multiplicity. Classical neo-Platonism, it is true, had the soul turn away from multiplicity in seeking Divine perfection, but this always involved finding the true self, and never was there a hint of a "wilderness" as the highest awareness of the Divine. Eckhart, like Plotinus and Augustine before him, finds the avenue to Divine understanding to be through a seeking and a finding of the center and essential nature of the soul. For Eckhart, however, perfection in God (and, in man, the finding of the Divine nature) involves disinterest, emptiness, quietude, nothingness, wilderness, and alienation. We have represented here a powerful and a novel advance over neo-Platonism in conceiving Divine perfection.

If to a systematically minded philosopher Eckhart seems vague and unconstructed, Nicolas Cusanus' fifteenth-century writings, though they bear a close family resemblance to the core of Eckhart's ideas about perfection, are developed in more technical detail. *Of Learned Ignorance* is perhaps the classical expression of negative theology, a method stressed by and associated with an extremely transcendental concept of perfection. "Enlightened ignorance" is Nicolas' extension of traditional negative theology, and, of course, at its roots it springs partly from the famed "Socratic ignorance" and partly from the biblical insistence that God may never be seen. Understanding that we cannot, and why we cannot, realize our desire to see God means for Cusanus acquiring an ignorance that is learned, i.e., an understanding of exactly why the desired goal is an impossibility. To realize the final impossibility of knowledge—this itself requires considerable understanding as to why the Divine perfection raises God above our grasp. To know why you cannot know God fully is in some sense to have grasped the Divine nature. For this reason the ignorance is "learned."

Cusanus makes unity identical with the absolute maximum, a traditional neo-Platonic feature, but it is this unity which places the study of God above reason. Yet, like the Plotinian One, this absolute maximum is the reconciliation of opposites and contains all at the same time that it is one, since the normal laws of distinction do not apply to it. This is something which cannot rationally be fully grasped—and thus our ignorance. But the more profoundly we understand the reason for our ignorance the closer we are to truth itself. Here one is reminded of the dialectic behind Anselm's ontological argument, and Cusanus uses Anselm's phrase, "that than which nothing greater can exist." To understand why the phrase is inadequate is to transcend the phrase and its structure. By argument you have been brought closer to God, even if it means abandoning the original concept of rational comprehension. "Learned ignorance" is unintelligible unless it is understood as a (non-Hegelian) dialectical process—acquiring knowledge, realizing the inadequacy of formulation and rational grasp, and so on without end.

The coincidence of opposites in Cusanus' First Principle is evident in his doctrine that the minimum is identified with the maximum. It is true that in pre-Socratic thought we can find ontology which works by the contrast of opposites, but we must wait until modern thought before we find the assertion of the identity of these opposing concepts. Plotinus places the principles of all things together without distinction in his One, but the assertion of their identity by Cusanus is another step. Like Plotinus, however, Cusanus finds distinctions only on a lower ontological level, among things which are susceptible of "more" and "less." And this leads Cusanus to a doctrine of the realization of all possible perfections in the First—or, rather, it is this doctrine which requires that the absolute maximum be all things and yet none of them, at once the maximum and the minimum. Thus we see that it is not some original pious sanctity which causes Cusanus to assert his ultimate ignorance about God, but actually a quite clear apprehension of the Divine nature which leads him to see the logical impossibility of making the First an item of knowledge.

No classical theory had made a strict contradiction applicable to God. Cusanus does, because he is rationalist enough to refuse to suspend the laws of logic. The complexity of the Divine as the ultimate source of all leads him to make statements which are opposed to each other. Were he to surrender logic in the sense of discursive thought at this point, as Plotinus tends to do, then he might not be driven so firmly toward a doctrine of learned ignorance. Strangely enough, it is his extreme rationalism, his refusal to surrender the distinctions necessary to reason, which forces him to place God beyond knowledge. Cusanus says that there is no difference between these two statements: "God is light" and "God is light at its lowest." Thus logic is driven into silence when it apprehends God, because it can neither surrender the distinctions necessary to its life nor reconcile the opposed statements.

Our rational process is not able to reconcile contradictions, and the fullness of all possible statements which Cusanus finds that he must make about God, as cause of all of the natural order, leads to an impossible combination of necessary attributes. It is precisely this clear vision of the ultimate complexity of God which places Him beyond our understanding, not our inability to apprehend Him. Only one who actually apprehends God can have a full appreciation of the difficulty in knowing Him in any definitive way. God's perfection, as locus of all possible perfections, is fully intelligible yet recognized as beyond our comprehension. If Cusanus could transcend discursive reason and find another mode of knowing, he might overcome his resultant ignorance, but, unlike Plotinus and Dionysius, he cannot.

Here we begin to find a concept of unity that makes it compatible with variety, as the actuality of all that is possible. For Cusanus it is the full realization, and the ontological priority, of the possibles, which leads him to reshape the limitations of classical ontology. Nonbeing is made identical with the maximum, since it is a possible form of existence. Unity, equality, and connection are made a trinity of concepts through which one can grasp the First. Such a unity is the modified unity (i.e., one which contains within its definition a relation to multiplicity) which Plato prefers in his *Parmenides*. Mathematical concepts become important for understanding things Divine; symbols, of course, become the sole possible approach to a knowledge of God's nature. A doctrine of the nature of God such as this is always behind a preference for symbolic knowledge, in virtue of which symbols are not only an appropriate approach but a necessity.

The Divine perfection is clearly conceived by Cusanus as the infinite actualization of all that is simply and absolutely possible. Absolute possibility and infinite actual existence are perfectly identified. The very scope of such a concept itself is what necessitates the ignorance at the end of the knowing process. Even contradictions are encompassed by God, which is another stumbling block in reason's way. This leads naturally to a preference for negative theology, where negative propositions can be true but affirmative propositions can in the nature of the case never be adequate. Our final position is to see that such a nature exists but also to see that, precisely because of what we know about it, we cannot comprehend it. The seeds of transformation in ontological structure, planted by the early theological interest in infinity, have gradually produced a change in ontological concepts until they seem to have completed a radical transformation with Eckhart and Cusanus.

Possibility becomes absolutely central and is asserted to descend from eternal unity, when previously it was precisely the demand for unity as a Divine perfection which excluded possibility. Cusanus asserts that we must begin by studying possibility, whereas Aristotle had insisted on the absolute priority of actuality, both for ontology and for the process of knowledge. Absolute possibility is God, a statement which now has meaning in the light of the ontological development but which would have shocked classical Greek thought. The so-called "modern" period which follows will actually revert to a more conservative and traditional ontological framework; but, whenever the centrality of theory of knowledge is overcome, the argument must proceed from the radical developments in ontology wrought at the close of the Middle Ages. Although overlooked during the "modern" period, the late Middle Ages (that era so often spurned as sterile and rigid) itself contains the formulation of contemporary ontological problems.

6

SPINOZA

AND

LEIBNIZ

With Scotus and Ockham a new view of Divine perfection, highly illuminating in the altered solutions it made possible to classical problems, had begun to emerge. Strangely enough, with the divorce between philosophy and theology that soon occurred, modern philosophers who treated theological questions reverted to much more traditional theological views. Spinoza's philosophy is radical in some respects, but in its view of Divine perfection it is quite traditional, almost reactionary. Leibniz incorporates some of the new emphasis upon the contingent and the possible, but in his final solution he is very close to the Thomistic view of the necessary process of selection by which the Divine nature is bound. Divine will is rejected as an important factor by Spinoza and Leibniz, and both Divine and human action thus become subjected to a rational necessity.

Perhaps Spinoza's most crucial statement is his identification of reality with perfection: "By reality and perfection I understand the same thing" (*Ethics,* Pt. II, Def. VI). It is true that all classical thought had associated perfection with the actual, but here a further step is taken and perfection is *identified* with the actual. The result is the elimination of any room for possible, but unrealized, entities. All reality now becomes part of the Divine nature, embraced in necessity and fully actualized under eternity's perspective. God's own existence had always been conceived as necessary and purged of potentiality, but here both God and the world are embraced by actuality, and reality is equated with perfection. The doctrine of infinite attributes becomes necessary (in place of possible worlds in the Divine mind) in order not to limit the Divine nature.

God, or substance, has for Spinoza the usual primary attribute of necessary existence, expressed as "cause-of-itself." This places substance in contrast with all particular things, the cause for each of which must be located in another being. Not only is substance infinite in a particular kind (i.e., thought), but it is absolutely infinite, which makes extension necessarily a part of the Divine nature. This no longer involves God in potentiality, since lack of fulfillment does not exist in an infinite perspective, a perspective which Spinoza and his God can adopt, as against Aristotle who could neither conceive of such a viewpoint nor conceive of the ontology which it makes possible. Freedom, of course, can now only mean necessity (the way of most classical thought), since no unrealized possibles exist; and such freedom is a goal not presently attained by any individual. Freedom remains, but only in the sense that it means "determined to action by itself alone," a definition which applies primarily to God—and to finite beings to the degree that, their understanding improved, they come to view themselves as part of an absolutely infinite substance.

There could be only one such substance, so that in this sense the traditional perfection of unity is maintained, although it is a unity containing absolute variety within it. Everything is ultimately understood adequately only through God, which preserves God as the traditional object of wisdom's quest, although understanding such a God involves a grasp of the world's complexity at the same time. God's actions are free, in the sense that no external force can compel him, but there are no alternatives to our present mode of actualization.

"Creation" is really eliminated as a concept, and Spinoza's reversion is to something very much like the Plotinian necessary emanation. God could not be without His effects, since His very nature includes them and there are no alternative sets of possibles. Contingency, usually kept out of the Divine nature, is now eliminated completely not only from God but from individual things as well. "Will" becomes only reason's tendency to accept a true idea and is a necessary cause. Some earlier philosophers had tried to keep contingency out of the Divine nature and yet allow some measure of freedom to man, and a few had even tried to allow God a small amount of freedom and man a little less. Within Spinoza's thought structure we see Scotus' maxim applied with a vengeance: if there is no contingency in the First Cause in causing there is no contingency in any second cause in acting. For in Spinoza's thought, both God and men are equally embraced by the necessity which perfection demands. The Divine will, to which theologians often appeal in order to introduce contingency, Spinoza dismisses as the refuge of ignorance.

Imperfection in man remains only in the form of inadequate ideas and as the passive emotions which these necessarily involve. God's perfection may still be distinguished from that of the finite, since God's ideas are fully adequate. Considered under the aspect of eternity, He is involved in no passive emotions. Sorrow as a passive emotion, then, becomes the mark of the imperfect, so that the Divine perfection is characterized by a lack of all emotion, except the joy which accompanies God's intellectual love (i.e., through man's comprehension in adequate ideas) of Himself.

Primary among the perfections of substance is its full actuality, that is, its existence as the adequate cause of all things and thus its freedom from suffering or the possession of passive emotions. In contrast, our human minds act at times and at times suffer. The perfection of God, or substance, frees it from such imperfection, because it is the adequate cause of every existing thing. Were there any being or action of which God could not be said to be the immediate cause, then He too would be subject to sorrow and passive emotions, because of His inability to conceive these through His own nature alone. Men are imperfect only in the sense of their not yet enlightened perspective of the causal nexus. Their understanding of their existence is merely a part of substance, in contrast to the goal of understanding the whole.

God, of course, strives for nothing, since all possibles are in existence, or become actual when viewed under the aspect of eternity, and He needs nothing outside of Himself to persevere in His being. Our need of external objects keeps us subject to emotions and causes us to call things "good" and "evil" as they help or hinder our continued mode of existence. God's perfection, being equated with what is real, has no such needs, since nothing exists outside of substance. The life of God, or substance, is entirely an internal affair, without alternative, devoid of passive emotion and, since self-contained and adequately conceived, neither good nor evil, but simply what it is.

Spinoza certainly stresses the unlimited aspect of Divine perfection, extending God's nature as he does infinitely beyond conception in his famous doctrine of infinite attributes. We know only two of these, thought and extension, but we do not limit God's nature by the boundaries of our ability to think. Not only is God infinite in kind, as, for example, in Thomas' infinity of form. Substance is absolutely infinite, which makes absolutely every kind of being a part of God. Here matter is taken up into the Divine nature as a part of it, no longer the destroyer of perfection because of its potentialities. The famed potentialities, usually thought to be necessarily present in matter, may now be brought under conception, since there is an idea paralleling every mode of extension. The Divine nature is different in kind from our world, but only in the sense that it includes the attributes of our known world as only two from among an actual infinity of attributes.

Nothing is indefinite save as, when viewed by human passive emotion, obscure understanding makes it appear so. Nothing is indeterminate, except as our understanding does not adequately grasp the causes which are operative. Potentiality reflects only an inadequate mode of comprehension, which disappears when things are viewed under the aspect of eternity. Nothing is self-sufficient except substance taken as a whole, which means that an essential dependency of existence still characterizes all finite modes. Motion is a part of God, but this does not imply an imperfection, since all is seen as realized when it is viewed under eternity.

Freedom becomes only a lack of external restriction, and does not exist in the sense of alternative routes of action. This restricts freedom to a property belonging only to God, or to ourselves when we are viewed as part of God; and this equates freedom with necessity. Time still characterizes the existence of all modes, but all entities may also be seen under the timeless perspective of eternity, which is man's rational and ethical goal. Plurality is without limit and is placed within the Divine nature, but unity is preserved through the existence of only one such substance. No ultimate chaos is to be found, inadequacy of understanding being the only remaining source of indeterminacy. Ultimately, nothing may elude reason's grasp or obscure any aspect of the absolutely infinite nature of substance.

Evil and good both disappear in God, being present only as the result of our finite need for things outside of ourselves. God's power is perfect and fully realized, restrained from full actualization by nothing, and ultimately identical with substance's self-understanding. Knowledge is the supreme characteristic of substance, but finite creatures may become Divine through sharing in this perfect causal understanding, open to them (as it was not in most previous views) without theoretical barriers. Substance alone is perfect as being cause-of-itself, but it is no more transcendent that it is immanent, although it certainly is both. Non-being has no ultimate role here, since all being is ultimately actualized without remainder. Nothing lacks being in so far as it is actual, and the only lack of actuality which appears is not ultimate but merely the result of inadequate understanding, the causes for which we can now delineate and comprehend.

Creation merely means temporal coming into being, never a radical origin, since God's decrees are part of His nature and are co-eternal with Him. Distinction is certainly present within a Divine nature that embraces the natural world as a part, but division is prevented by the absolutely infinite reach of substance and the full reality of all possibles. God's nature does not require that the negative approach be used, since our minds, as part of the infinite intellect of God, participate in God's own understanding of Himself.

Leibniz is most popularly known for his *Monadology,* but it is primarily in his *Theodicy* that one must look to find his view of the Divine perfection. It is true that, as a condensation, the *Monadology* contains glimpses of his doctrine, but it is chiefly in justifying the ways of God to man in creation (the theme of theodicy) that the nature of Divine perfection is best clarified. For God's action in creation can neither be explained nor accounted for except by reference to the nature of His perfection. Freedom and evil are facts which can only be interpreted by reference to the concept of God's goodness, which is the operation of His nature as perfect. And Leibniz' task here is a modern one, since the explanation of God's choice in creation is only a meaningful question within an ontology in which possibles exist beyond those actualizable in this world. The traditional limitation of possibility (to merely the potential within the structure we find actualized) has with Leibniz been set aside once and for all.

Like Thomas, Scotus, and Ockham, Leibniz takes the metaphysically possible to be limited by nothing other than the law of non-contradiction. This being the case—and admitting the non-actuality of at least part of any such an absolutely infinite set—the problem of theodicy is posed: to account for God's selection in such a way as to make the existence of evil in the actualized world compatible with God's goodness. Unlike Plato's gods, who are made responsible only for the good (which is essentially the neo-Platonic and Augustinian answer, too), God must be made to account for *all* that we find actual, including what men call good and what they call evil. When no other world but our own is possible (as for Spinoza), the problem is less severe. When the high Middle Ages lifts the restrictions upon the possibles in God's knowledge, then the concept of Divine perfection becomes more difficult and also more important.

Leibniz' answer, although posed within a modern ontological framework, is essentially traditional and conservative. As they were for Thomas, the alternative possibles are really possible only logically. The goodness of God and the possibles, when taken together, are such as to permit only the actualization of our present constellation. When both Thomas and Leibniz say that God might have created a better world, they speak purely hypothetically; actual reference to the nature of God and His perfection requires what we in fact find present. This is the basis for the famous doctrine of the best of all possible worlds. Traditional ontologies knew of no possible worlds other than ours (save perhaps a few hints to be found in the pre-Socratics). Leibniz expands the possibles, but his conservative view of Divine perfection leads him to the same practical outcome that the traditionalists took for granted as their starting point.

In the preface to the *Theodicy* Leibniz glimpses a more novel solution to the problem when he says that the perfections of God are as those of our soul, for it has not usually been to the soul that the tradition had turned for its model of Divine perfection. However, a necessitarian view of human action (ironically enough, originally a consequence necessitated by a different view of Divine perfection) soon robs Leibniz' model of any potential radicalism. Predestination rules the *Monadology*, which seems to be a necessity for the modern rationalist, and God then surely cannot escape to action which is based on a decision between genuine alternatives. To be sure, the doctrine of the possibles has provided logical alternatives for Divine action, but God's mode of action upon them in original creative choice is the element which still yields the classical necessity we find present in our world, in our actions, and also in God's.

God pre-establishes the truth (i.e., the form) of future events in establishing their causes. Yet very early Leibniz claims to hold to a balance between liberty and absolute necessity and to establish an indifference in freedom. However, the fine print in the contract must be read here before one hails this document as a metaphysical basis for human liberty, such as might be found in Scotus and Ockham. For the freedom Leibniz provides consists in establishing the existence of a realm of logically non-contradictory possibles, which stand in contrast to the actuality of our world; but it does not consist in alternatives which are still allowable even from the standards which God's perfection demands as a basis for His choice. Pre-established harmony governs our actual world, just as it governs God's original act in creation. Leibniz rejects Spinoza's "geometrical" necessity as a perfection governing God; but he substitutes a logical possibility of alternatives, which, when coupled with the necessary criteria, combine to make it necessary that a certain set of possibles be selected.

The principle of "universal harmony" is perhaps most important in Leibniz' conception of perfection, for it is a harmony that excludes the actualization of any possibles which are not compossible, i.e., capable of simultaneous existence without logical—and also, apparently, actual—contradiction. Of course, this requires "intelligence" as a primary perfection in God as the First Principle, since reasoning among possibles is required for creation in a way it never was in neo-Platonism. "Will" is also a primary and irreducible perfection, since actualization means the attachment of power, through an act of will, to some possibles and not to others. "Infinity," of course, is a perfection and, as for all moderns, troubles Leibniz not in the least. It is possible for him to understand and deal with infinity in a way which would have startled Aristotle.

Goodness as a perfection requires that God choose the best set from among the possibles, and God would be imperfect, i.e., correctable by man, if it were not so. Why, then, is there physical and metaphysical evil? Although there is an infinity of possible worlds, Leibniz answers, all of them contain some evil, so God has not the choice of avoiding evil by actualizing another conceivable world. And His will is determined by goodness, so that God actualizes according to the proportion of good contained (this being determined by a fixed, single scale), a world without evil being impossible. But God cannot create another God; therefore all creatures contain limitations and possess only certain degrees of perfection. Here Leibniz distinguishes certainty from necessity and introduces the doctrine of the "inclination" of the will. The course of the will is *certain,* being inclined by the nature of the possibles, but it is not *necessary* since other possibles than those He is certain to actualize are logically real.

Contingency enters into this scheme only in the sense that alternative courses of action are logically consistent and conceivable, but there is a sufficient reason for every actualization that makes its route and result certain. Prevailing inclination always triumphs; contingency remains real because the existence of logically real possibles eliminates the absolute necessity involved in allowing ontological existence to nothing other than our world and its potentialities. Even the imperfections in the universe which God actually constituted do not imply that it is not better than every other possible universe. The best of the possibles have been actualized, God acting as a perfect cause. Some evil is present in any possible universe; and some imperfection of parts may be required for a greater perfection of the whole, our limited perspectives obstructing our comprehending this at times.

Imperfection comes from necessary limitations, which means that no creation can be accomplished without imperfection. Yet, what we have is the greatest variety possible within the simplest basic plan. Greater variety would bring certain advantages but reduce the advantage of simplicity. Thus God's perfection acting in creation struck a compromise here, and our resulting world is the best possible, considering the balancing of criteria which was and is necessary. Taken in part, our world might be better; but when all the criteria are taken as a whole, we see the goodness of the possibles inclining the Divine will toward the particular action which He in fact took, although not as if other unrealized possibles were not very much in His view.

This blend in Leibniz of the traditional necessity in perfection with the expansion of the field of possibles to an absolute infinity is curious indeed. His ontological framework is radically altered, but the classical limitation of God to one course of action remains. Thomas put a traditional stress on necessity but allowed an ontological expansion of the possibles in the Divine nature. Leibniz, like a true modern, begins with the possibles (anything being conceivable and therefore possible that does not involve a contradiction), but he nonetheless views God's perfection as requiring necessary selection and predestination. Infinity is surely a ruling concept in perfection, as against the early tradition, and God's nature is not fully actual but contains more possibles than could ever be realizable. The denial of full actuality does not demean God's perfection, as it might have traditionally, since His choice in actualization remains ultimately a necessary one.

Motion is thus eliminated, which might have been introduced into the Divine nature by a doctrine of the possibles. Freedom is present as the existence of logical alternatives, although necessity still governs choice. Plurality must have a higher status in such a concept of perfection, although never the plurality of choice, since this remains singular. Evil is placed among the possibles in the Divine nature, a modern innovation; but the necessary criteria which govern choice and the maximization of compatible goods removes any possible reproach from God. (Job misunderstands the lack of choice really open to Divine action and God's necessity to compromise in any creation.) God is infinitely powerful, but His power is exercised only under necessary guidance. What is compossible we have. More than that neither God can do nor man can ask of action so rationally restricted.

7

KANT

AND

HEGEL

Nearly every major form of contemporary philosophical theology can either directly or indirectly trace at least one part of its ancestry to Kant or Hegel. Kant's fatherhood belongs to those who abstain from metaphysical construction in theology and to those who begin their constructive work either with a theory of knowledge or with an epistemological prolegomenon designed to apologize for its possibility. For symbolic convenience, even those who trace their origins to Hume can be counted under the negative and empirical side of Kant's critical method. Although it may have lacked philosophical assistance in its constructive efforts, theology has not lacked attention since the time of Hume and Kant. Perhaps most characteristic of this epoch has been the continued effort expended on the preliminaries of philosophical theology. The old question has been posed in new ways, i.e., whether the construction of a doctrine of the Divine nature is possible.

"Kantians of the first *Critique*" (i.e., those who stress the primacy of that volume) are closely akin to Hume's empirically-minded heirs in insisting on the priority of, if not the exclusive preoccupation with, epistemological and logical questions. Thus, a great deal of theology has become a uniquely modern form of apologetics and finds it difficult if not impossible to return to the speculative and constructive task. Much theology of the past hundred years has found itself unable to escape from Kant's paralyzing methodological criticism, and this accounts for the comparative scarcity of genuinely creative and constructive theologies (other than those carrying to completion the fruitful suggestions of the nineteenth century). Here the theological and metaphysical apologists are mirror images of their empirical critics, wishing to come to different conclusions but asking essentially the same questions. Perhaps nothing has been more healthy and at the same time more stultifying in its effect upon constructive effort than the empirical critique launched by Hume, supported by one side of Kant and continued in the present age by several schools.

"Kantians of the second *Critique*" have largely been responsible for the ethical basis which some recent theology has adopted, as well as the predominant value orientation characteristic of much current philosophical thought. If epistemological questions have paralyzed direct discussions of the Divine nature, this line of thought argues, then perhaps theology can be constructed upon and oriented by a primarily ethical basis. Undoubtedly Kant is here influenced by the Reformation, which once again stressed the ethical side of Christianity as opposed to its philosophical and speculative side. But whatever its origins, the group who follow Kant here have found it possible to construct theologies within an ethical framework, even when they continued to feel skeptical about the possibility of any direct knowledge of the Divine nature. Since Kant published the second *Critique,* much theology has become simply a general ethical theory, but its major problem has been, and still is, to escape the domination of mere local custom and provincial ethical standards.

"Kantians of the third *Critique*" are a much rarer species. Even dedicated Kantians admit that the third *Critique* is Kant's most difficult writing to interpret, and yet it is here that the connection is to be made with Hegel, and it is here that the speculative side of Kant appears. The third *Critique* contains some suggestion of the possibility of transcending the forms and categories which limit our mode of knowledge. More important, it is here that the possibility appears for some direct knowledge of the self as a noumenal entity. Previously Kant had allowed metaphysics to be actual merely as a natural disposition of reason, not as a constructed doctrine, and God was to be known only indirectly through the requirements of the ethical life. But with the third *Critique* as a basis, it seems possible to find a ground for direct statement about the Divine nature, but this positive and constructive suggestion by Kant has largely come to be identified with its Hegelian development.

The empirical side of Kant may be used to explain the discontinuance of the classical questions about Divine perfection which is characteristic of so much of the contemporary scene. And the ethical side of Kant may be given as an explanation of the almost complete transformation of much theological thought into theoretical and practical ethics. Thus, when the question of Divine perfection is raised, it stands in a more tenuous context in the present era than it ever did in most pre-eighteenth-century discussion. There are contemporary constructive efforts today, most of which can be traced to Hegel. But, if the time is ripe for a revival of speculative theological and metaphysical effort, it is to the great centuries of constructive work beginning with the Greeks that one must turn in order not to be either immobilized by the Humian and Kantian critique or prejudiced in approach and in the formulation of the issues by the unparalleled dominance which Hegel has come to have over constructive thought. An historical revival is necessary in order to restore a needed balance to theological method and to free it from the domination of modes of thought which are merely recent.

Perhaps Hegel's view of Divine perfection can best be grasped by comparing it with Plotinus' doctrine. As was noted before, if Plato's model of perfection is the level of existence given to the forms, it is characteristic that Plotinus begins his analysis with the soul. Considering Kant's epistemological skepticism, it is interesting that the soul is also Hegel's starting point and constant model. But Hegel is not merely a modern day Plotinian. Plotinus, discovering a governing principle of unity within the soul's life, extracts this as the model of perfection, leaving the soul in its full life to occupy a lower level in the Divine hierarchy. Thus reason is transcended and is not Plotinus' ultimate guide. Hegel, however, preserves the ideal soul as his model of perfection and thus never arrives at pure unity or transcends reason. Hegel always retains the distinctions of thought as his guide.

This explains Hegel's distinctive revolution in the doctrine of Divine perfection, namely the introduction of motion as not only compatible with but necessarily characteristic of Divinity. It must not be overlooked that there are times when Plotinus describes the One as if it contained movement, but the important point is that distinction and the rationality of thought are for Plotinus necessarily transcended in the ultimate sphere. The rationality of the pattern of the self's development is only a starting point, not a model, for Plotinus; for Hegel the depth of the self's existence is itself the key. For Hegel the pattern of Divine activity can be traced and comprehended rationally, and motion becomes absolutely necessary to the proper understanding of the Divine life. Inclusiveness and relations are with Hegel made central to perfection. These can be attained or grasped rationally, never as at rest but only through a process.

For Plotinus it is safe to say that motion is characteristic of all that proceeds from the One but is not ultimately constitutive of the One itself. It is otherwise with Hegel. If we need an historical location, Hegel as well as any figure can serve as a symbol for the elevation of motion to become a primary characteristic of Divine perfection. Rational development now characterizes both the perfect and the imperfect. In fact, the development of the latter is to be understood as the self-expression of the former, without which it would remain unfulfilled and thus unself-conscious and imperfect. The Absolute has to be conceived essentially as a result, Hegel tells us in the *Phenomenology*. This is as radical a change in the concept of perfection as has ever been attempted, and the contemporary scene is almost totally under the spell cast by this novelty.

The Absolute is to be represented as Spirit. If this is to remain its ultimate perfection, then it will require the development of a complete and fully rational system, in order for its perfection to be realized and in order for the mind to understand it adequately. When ontological perfection was devoid of motion, propositions could be true independently of one another, but coherence and system come to be required as the criteria of truth when what is ontologically ultimate and perfect is also necessarily in motion. Where scientific knowledge was concerned, Aristotle defined substance as universal form; now Hegel defines its essence as subject, and the self becomes the source in which a doctrine of perfection must be found. Since no self remains self-identical, only a system which grasps and represents both change and opposition can express truth. Being has the character of self, is motion.

The basis of a philosophy of organism is here propounded, and this means that thought can be both systematic and comprehensive only if it duplicates the organic process of motion, here seen as constitutive of perfection itself. The very nature of understanding is to be a process, and this does not, as it does for Aquinas, reflect our inadequate modes of knowing but rather merely reflects the nature of Divine life. Nor is reason transcended in the quest for perfection, since the total process may be dialectically grasped. What is rational is the rhythm of the organic whole. Our world and selves represent the process of the Absolute becoming "conscious of itself," so that the processes of our world and lives become necesarily a part of the understanding of Divine perfection. Consciousness, selfhood, and rationality are not transcended but are exalted, since motion and process are now compatible with perfection. In fact, Spirit is real only as the moving process of the aspects which it possesses.

God has existence in nature as well as in spirit, which is reminiscent of Spinoza's view of thought and extension as the two primary attributes of substance or God. However, Spinoza keeps one side of God traditionally motionless. He identifies the ideal of perfection (and thus of rationality and of the ethical life) with God as motionless, i.e., as viewed under the aspect of eternity. Like Spinoza, Hegel not only includes the process of the world within the Divine life as its necessary expression, but he makes the process essentially characteristic of the Divine life and thus makes his God more centrally a person than could ever have been true for Spinoza. In comprehensiveness, inclusiveness, and the ultimacy of rationality Spinoza and Hegel are alike; however Spinoza retains the classical view of the motionless vision of the Divine perspective while Hegel transforms the Divine life itself, modeling it after the pattern of the human self.

Like Augustine, Hegel finds God by starting from his own consciousness; unlike Augustine this starting point also serves as the primary norm for Divine perfection. The incarnation in a human self of such a Divinity, of course, is not only easily conceivable but becomes almost necessary to the complete self-development of such a God. The Divine nature is intuitively apprehended as being the same as the human, since Hegel begins with self-consciousness as Kant could not do. When the absolute Being exists as a concrete actual self-consciousness, this is not an essentially difficult concept as it was for the previous tradition; for such a Being must come so to exist in order to attain its highest nature. Individual self-consciousness, taken as the starting point and the norm for perfection, now requires of God individual and self-conscious existence for the completion of Divine perfection. This is true of all history and is not confined to one moment.

God is revealed, and is only real, as Spirit. Thus movement is compatible with perfection as the necessary expression of absolute Being as a Spirit. Not to grasp absolute Being as Spirit is to grasp nothing. This, of course, leads to the important Hegelian notion of the rationality, the necessity, and the perfection of opposition, of struggle and of progress through cancellation. This we know to be the inmost nature of the self, to struggle with opposing tendencies and to bring them to resolution, and this process, in its perfect expression, now becomes God's life. As otherness, and thus opposition, are part of any conscious self, so they now become Divine attributes and are made perfect. God's perfection consists in maintaining self-identity in the face of the negative and its resulting opposition. Such conflict results from uniting the abstract with the concrete, a process which both Spinoza and Hegel insist on as necessary for Divinity, although in different ways.

God's life as perfect must include the particular and opposed aspects of individual existence, hence the Divine life comes to actuality through process and struggle. The abstract must include the other than itself, the concrete particular. Only a process could make God to be God (i.e., perfect or fulfilled) under these circumstances. Unity is maintained as a classical hallmark of perfection, since distinctions and oppositions are in the form of moments which are overcome and included in the fully realized process. Alienation is as much a part of the Divine nature as it is of human nature. Evil is not opposed to the Divine nature but is a part of its necessary impetus to full self-consciousness. As for Spinoza, nothing can be external to absolute Being, which means that every aspect of individual existence must become a moment in the realization of its own perfection.

Truth is not a state or a statement but a process, a rational movement. The moments as much *are* as they *are not,* and this is the character of thought and the process which is Spirit. The unity here is to be found in the fact that distinctions and oppositions appear merely as moments, transcended in the fully realized self-consciousness. Even God must be reconciled with His own existence, which means that He must lose abstractness and alienation through incarnation and death. This movement through its whole self constitutes the actual reality of God, without which He could not attain perfection. It is through action that Spirit is Spirit, so it must be through historical action that God becomes God. When one reads Hegel he comes to realize the truth of the maxim: There is nothing new under the sun—since the time of Hegel.

God can only come to know Himself through process, which is accomplished as actual history. And this brings out another side of Hegelian ontology which has perhaps dominated theology even more thoroughly than his metaphysical conception of perfection as process (a basic idea which all later process and organismic metaphysicians merely borrow as a theme and elaborate upon). For it is in Hegel that we must find the primary force that has driven part of philosophy and most of theology into historical and cultural analysis. This is a perfectly obvious consequence of Hegel's view of the nature of the Divine existence. If God becomes perfect (i.e., complete) and self-conscious only through the unfolding of historical and natural phenomena, then it is logical to turn to history, to sociology, to psychology, to the arts and to literature and to expect to find unfolded there profound theological insight.

When God's life was more detached from the actions of nature and of men, the theological and metaphysical task was in a real sense much easier. Would it be an exaggeration to pin a century of fantastic effort expended in historical and cultural analysis onto an idea of Hegel? Surely it would be impossible to account for the quantity of historical research and the intensity of the sociological and cultural inquiry if men did not hope to gain from it some profound understanding of ultimate reality, and this is possible only on Hegel's basic view of the nature of, and the approach which we must make to, God. It is Hegel and his descendants, then, who must be held responsible for the prominence of history and culture in recent theology, since neither Hume nor Kant nor the previous tradition provides any optimistic ground for such an interest. If process is not ultimately characteristic of the Divine nature and compatible with His perfection, then no study of process could hope to yield first principles for our understanding of God or man or the natural order.

Kant and Hume gave philosophical theology its methodological and its epistemologically absorbing concern, and Kant provided the possibility of a metaphysically agnostic theology based upon the ethical life. Hegel gave philosophy and theology good reason to be interested in the process of history as revelatory, and theology built on cultural and psychological analyses became a reality. Without the critical empiricism of Kant or Hegel's revised concept of Divine perfection, little of this revolution would have been possible. In contrast to the preceding twenty or twenty-five centuries, most theology and metaphysics since Kant and Hegel has been a variation on one or more of the basic themes which they formulated.

If Kant—at least in the side which he shares with Hume—can be held responsible for the abandonment of the traditional metaphysical questions in theology, it is Hegel who has fixed the concepts which are now basic to all subsequent constructive attempts (construction being contrasted with the revival of a traditional view). As far as infinity is concerned, few metaphysical arguments could appear to be so well settled at this point. Infinity now is the natural atmosphere of all theological work, and it is not only compatible with rationality but becomes reason's fullest and only free expression. But such infinity as characteristic of Divinity's nature and thought is neither indefinite nor incomplete, although its completion for Hegel involves its expression in the historical realm. At any moment it may be indeterminate, since the oppositions and particularities of human existence and consciousness are part of its life. The process involves overcoming these aspects of indeterminacy.

Potentiality has thus become compatible with perfection, since the actuality of Divinity is only achieved through actualizing the potentialities (including some actualized through opposition and destruction) of the historical and human world. However, in keeping with the tradition, Hegel never sacrifices the self-sufficiency of the Divine life. Its development is a necessary one (another classical feature), and it is essentially the process which determines the particulars, not the indeterminate individual moments which guide the self-realizing process. The process makes the particulars what they are, although it is true that the realization of perfection is possible only through the opposition inherent in individual moments; such conflict alone provides the passion from which flows the energy to actualize.

Freedom, as for Spinoza, is to be found in the self-realization of the whole of Spirit. By accepting what the process yields from its oppositional (i.e., dialectical) progress, the individual becomes truly himself and in that sense achieves freedom. Even if the theological and the metaphysical element is often missing, existentialism (e.g., Kierkegaard) can nevertheless be viewed as essentially Hegelian in its stress upon the necessity of, and the edification provided by, suffering. This is especially evident in the existentialist interest in the individual consciousness as the key to understanding our situation. All that is missing in existentialism is the transformation of this view of individual life into a rational and comprehensive doctrine of the expression and the development of Divine self-consciousness.

Unity is maintained by Hegel as a system, although plurality is given stress as individual moments without which the comprehensive development would have no material or life force. Chaos, as in most classical views, is banished and form made compatible (as in Aquinas) with infinity and now (in Hegel) also with process. Power is most certainly central to perfection in such a concept as Hegel's, and one finds a strange affinity here to that important but undeveloped passage in Plato's *Statesman* where power is identified with being. Since rationality always characterizes such a comprehensive and partially destructive process, knowledge remains a primary perfection of the Divine. Here motion does not deny the possibility of a rigorous science, as it would for Aristotle, but instead completes it. Being and non-being are equally ultimate and both are compatible with perfection, since these basic opposites provide the very source of opposition, and thus also of power and motion.

Transcendence characterizes Divine perfection, but only the transcendence of any particular view, person, or historical moment, never the transcendence of reason as incapable of comprehending the dialectics of the total process. Surely the Divine is also perfectly immanent in the world, since its self-consciousness and thus its perfection can only be achieved through individual consciousness and the unfolding of historical process. Simplicity, however, must be excluded by Hegel as a classical characteristic of perfection, since process requires inclusiveness and the most comprehensive becomes, as it does for Spinoza, the most real. The union of the most abstract with the greatest (even if conflicting) concrete detail is now the essence of perfection. However, although this certainly requires distinction within the Divine nature, division (as in all classical treatment) is ruled out, due to the power and the absolute control which the Divine exercises over its own development.

Interestingly enough, both positive and negative attribution become equally necessary for such a view, whereas most classical theories used either positive attribution or negative predication only as a means to, or in place of, a finally positive characterization. And the world must have come into being, i.e., be subject to creation and not be eternal, since the eternality of any framework without development is inconceivable. Perhaps Hegel, not Darwin, is really responsible for the grip which evolutionary thought has upon the contemporary mind. Furthermore, the Divine life involves the actualization of entities not all compossible, since from such opposition comes the very power of its actualization. What is good, therefore, must be plural, and the conflict of standards of value is, consequently, both ultimate and necessary for perfection.

When it comes to language, it is obvious that Hegel sides with univocation (as contrasted with equivocation or the method of analogy). Since the Divine life is essentially so like the human personality, human terms and concepts will obviously be highly appropriate. Since it is through self-consciousness that God becomes known, there will be no inappropriateness in the use of essentially psychological categories to characterize Divinity. The attributes of personality are not excluded from perfection as incompatible but are taken as the very key to its understanding. The same essential process which governs our individual consciousness, opposition, conflict, and even destruction, is the same process (expanded to include nature, logic, and science) through which God's perfection becomes actualized, i.e., comes to full self-consciousness.

Hegel knew, of course, that prosaic and sordid human history did not express the Divine life, and he saw this with a clarity which those influenced by him have often forgotten. Insight comes only from history, idealized (i.e., philosophically transformed) cultural and human self-consciousness. It is not really from cultural and historical *facts* that enlightenment flows, but rather from *ideal facts reconstructed* by philosophical method. The self must take its cultural and historical facts and transfigure them under reason's guidance in order to find significance in them. Factual, historical, and statistical inquiry into cultural phenomena will neither give insights into the Divine life nor yield any basis for certainty. Objective and factual history are as such uninteresting. But as reason begins the ideal reconstruction and interpretation, then, through reason's guided development, the Divinely perfect process will become visible as realized.

PART TWO

SOME
IMPORTANT
CONCEPTS
RELATED
TO
PERFECTION

INTRODUCTION TO PART TWO

In a contemporary constructive effort, how shall we employ historical materials and earlier theories? Is it possible to extract a crucial point from a complicated setting and then employ it in present discussion? What happens to a doctrine when it is lifted out of its native setting and used for analytical and constructive purposes? These are the questions which an historical-critical-speculative and constructive attempt must face.

What, let us ask, are our alternatives? If we must first complete a total historical source inquiry and reconstruction, that task will be impossible for any one man to accomplish (and perhaps impossible in theory) in order to go on to systematic work. Yet if we abandon historical material altogether, we risk cutting ourselves adrift, making ourselves more vulnerable to current whims. And more important, we cannot learn from, or train ourselves by, previous speculative thought unless we pick it up and use it. Metaphysics and theology have no training ground, no pre-established standards other than those to be found in the body of the writings of the great speculative thinkers. We must use historical sources for contemporary construction or starve for lack of theoretical food.

Furthermore, a close look at classical writers reveals an instructive fact: none of those men were by our exacting standards historical scholars, and yet all of them seemed to orient their own writing by constant reference to their predecessors. Whether overtly or not, most classical writers seem to be using and speaking to a variety of their speculative forebearers. It is interesting to note how many in the past and in the present (e.g., Plato, Aquinas, Spinoza, and Heidegger) claim to have received their orienting direction by reaching back and drawing on some past work. Contemporary theologians and metaphysicians must assert their right to the use of every historical source.

Even at the risk of generality, we must learn to *use* theories, in addition to knowing how to *analyze* their detail. These two enterprises, of course, should be kept distinct, and the employment of a theory should never be confused with a scholarly inquiry into its context. But both are needed for our speculative health. If we lack scholarship, we may distort or fundamentally misunderstand translated theories; if we do not make use of them in constructive attempts, then our own speculative powers grow weak from disuse or may be disoriented from their tradition. Neither must be lost or allowed to engage in damaging warfare with the other.

In the first part of this essay, a brief historical summary was attempted. It necessitated changing the theories in exact detail but, it is hoped, not in essence. In Part II a more difficult transition occurs, one which moves from historical theory toward a reconstructed solution. Admittedly it is sometimes hard to tell when the reference passes from someone else's theory to the author's own statement. Such, for instance, is the case in much of Aristotle's writing, interestingly enough particularly in his metaphysical writings. Metaphysics and theology seem to grow immediately out of previous theories, although not necessarily following any exact historical pattern.

When has a previous theory been left behind and a distinctively new theory emerged, capable of sustaining itself under analysis and expansion? That is the critical question which must be applied to every contemporary reworking of a classical issue. On the surface, the presence of historical fragments may seem confusing; actually it may be a more honest confession of source. As ever, the novel emerges from the familiar when the long familiar is reworked in new lights.

Chapters VI and VII evidence this process more clearly. The ordering and the priority given to concepts is in itself another standard measure of a man's view. Theories change as different concepts are raised from subordinate to central positions, and the theoretical result of this summary and reordering becomes evident in the last two chapters. Actually, the way in which any topic is approached, any material treated, is itself the most crucial fact about a theory or study. In that sense, the last two chapters simply bring to consciousness what the whole essay has unconsciously evidenced all along.

Most metaphysicians would fail if they had to stand on their historical accuracy. And yet the life of a metaphysical or theological theory is so tenuous that it must attach itself to previous theories or risk oblivion. Like Plato's form of unity, metaphysics has no visible existence—except in the body of writing which actually comprises it. Thus, the contemporary theoretician must use this accumulation and yet pass beyond mere commentary on it.

What, we must also ask, could be in the mind of a metaphysician when he commits a speculative sentence to print? Are we safe in assuming that he had a single specific meaning which an exact analysis can uncover? Does he use words as others in his time do, or does his theoretical mind give each crucial term a unique task? These most fundamental questions cannot be answered here, but the answer given to them is crucial to the way in which previous theological and metaphysical theories are used. If the metaphysician always operates at the limit of his understanding, necessarily and forever in a boundary situation, then the words he uses never lead to an exact formulation in the mind of anyone other than himself. They only lead on to further speculation. Metaphysical and theological words, then, may not be entities in themselves. They simply yield insight and further theories, which in turn provide additional perspective.

Speculative theories, whether concerning God or man, cannot be totally modern, since neither God nor man is. Nor can such theories stand alone or support themselves for longer than their speaker lasts, unless they tie themselves into the body of preserved literature. Some recent theories have been too novel and thus too rootless; others have never passed beyond scholarly inquiry to recreative efforts. The possibility of being simultaneously historical and contemporary, that the second part of this essay attempts to explore. Success would mean the beginning of a self-supporting and yet novel theoretical structure.

8

INFINITY

AND

UNITY

Perhaps in no other area of philosophy is cumulative progress more difficult to discern than in metaphysics. In some ways this is as it should be. Metaphysics seeks to delineate in words the basic structure encompassing nature and man, but this structure is not itself subject to change, even if the terms in which it is described are. Ethical conduct, for instance, as philosophical data is much better characterized by evolution than is metaphysical structure. The metaphysicians influenced by Hegel are perhaps the exceptions to this rule; for them all phenomena are somehow metaphysically important. Thus we have recently been passing through an era of metaphysical novelty—in terms, in concepts (e.g., Whitehead), and in novelty of viewpoint. Nevertheless, in historical perspective the "lexicon" found in Aristotle's *Metaphysics* still serves very well as a basic definition of both metaphysics and the terms important to it.

In spite of this relative stability, a metaphysician or theologian in our day is in a position to compare and contrast the virtues and vices, the advantages and the disadvantages, of historical metaphysical views, and to do so with a completeness and an accuracy perhaps hitherto unparalleled. A study of the Middle Ages leaves one impressed with the fruitfulness of that time, and this stands in contrast to the scarcity of the original metaphysical writings which were available for use in that age. The Enlightenment was by nature uninterested in the thought of preceding eras and suffered for its provincialism by a lack of perspective on its own views. The nineteenth century was profoundly interested in historical material, but it had a peculiar way of bending every view to make it fit into its prearranged place in a nineteenth-century architechtonic. Philosophy, if not theology, having broken so radically with nineteenth-century schemes, is left with the advantage of having recovered the historical sources which we are now free to study on their own terms.

One advantage in our possession of such a range of historical material, now freed from the transforming grasp of peculiarly nineteenth-century perspectives, can be seen in the concept of infinity as it relates to the question of the nature of Divine perfection. It is perfectly clear that Aristotle associates infinity with the indefinite and the indeterminate; and, as such, it is outside the grasp of knowledge. For him form means limitation and completion. The infinite or the unlimited stands opposed to both and is thus opposed to perfection, which requires limitation and completion. Only the potential infinite is allowed by Aristotle, but this can never be actualized, and actuality is the very hallmark of perfection. Plato does not make the unlimited a central concept, but he does make use of it at least in the *Philebus* in asserting that all things (perhaps even the Forms themselves) arise as a combination of the limited with the unlimited. From even this brief history the problem is clear: If infinity is to be compatible with perfection, then a mode of knowledge (either in God or in men) must be found which is capable of grasping it in totality. For this to be possible, a way must be found to reconcile infinity with form, or else to provide a mode of knowledge which is not dependent upon a grasp of form. In any case, infinity must be made fully actual and purged of its association with the incomplete and the indeterminate.

Aquinas represents just such a process of the purification of infinity, for he conceives it so that it is made compatible with form, actualized in God, and characteristic of the primary mode of Divine knowledge. Infinity is not transcended, except perhaps, as we shall see later, by unity. Aquinas retains the classical stress upon form as the condition for knowledge but makes it compatible with infinity. Such infinity may make the Divine nature impossible for us to comprehend, although not difficult to grasp, but the presence of form and the possession by God of an infinite mode of knowledge keep God's nature infinite without placing it beyond form or beyond all knowledge, although it is beyond man's natural mode of knowledge via form.

In an historical review of the use of "infinity," one thing quickly becomes clear: the concept is never discussed or applied to God simply by itself. Always the question is, "An infinity of what?" Yet the question of infinity naturally arises in connection with the Divine nature, since the Divine can be Divine only by being qualitatively different from the natural order. This was not always so, as we have seen in classical Greek thought, but most often it has been true. Especially since the Christian era, the method has been to apply to God in an infinite mode whatever qualities or attributes He is said to share with limited beings (e.g., power). Of course what it is important to note is that not all theologians agree to use terms applicable to human nature in their description of the Divine, particularly those who stress the Divine transcendence. Whoever does use terms to describe God's nature which also apply to the natural order, then, will find the application of the term in an infinite mode a natural tendency.

Spinoza, and perhaps Plotinus and Hegel, are the exceptions to this rule since they also apply infinity to the natural order. In fact, one characteristic tendency of modern thought seems to be the common acceptance of infinity as being widely applicable and easily handled. Descartes and Leibniz have no trouble grasping infinity, and when this is the case it is not too hard to see infinite aspects as present also within the natural order. Perhaps such ease in the use of infinity accounts for the problem modern thought seems to have of keeping God distinct from the natural world. This application of infinity to the natural order is most obvious in Spinoza's writing. The natural realm certainly has finite aspects, but infinity also applies both to nature's modes and to its attributes. However, the attributes of our known natural world are limited to two (extension and thought), and this raises the question of an infinity in kind vs. an absolute infinity.

This concern over the question of the possibility of an absolute infinity (i.e., an infinity of infinite kinds) is perhaps most characteristic of the modern temper. Aristotle considered the question of an actual infinite only in the category of quantity. Puzzled as he was about the necessity of admitting the infinite to be in some sense actual, he limited the question to one category and rejected even the consideration of the question of infinity as itself being infinite. Aristotle's theory of knowledge (in which knowledge is dependent upon form and form is made the very principle of limitation) prevented such an expansive consideration of the infinite's mode of existence. Modern rationalism, which considers it natural and normal to deal with infinites, raises the perfection which it applies to God above that of infinity in kind to that of the absolutely infinite.

Even if the natural world and the men in it can be said to possess aspects or kinds of infinity, or to be able to grasp them in knowledge, still the absolutely infinite characterizes God alone and is grasped by Him alone. From now on it is not simple infinity, but the kind of infinity, which distinguishes man from God. Yet a Divine nature characterized by such an expanded form of infinity does not transcent knowledge, since each of the infinite attributes is in itself knowable. The unity of such a nature becomes a kind of unity that is not opposed to distinction but instead comprehends every possible variety. Thus it is a unity due to the fact that nothing is outside its nature, rather than through any lack of internal distinctions. Reason, in expanding its grasp to an infinity of infinite kinds, has created a new kind of unity by which it is able to keep reason, which requires unity for its operation, ultimately applicable to every aspect of Divinity.

Excluding for the moment, then, those who make infinity as a Divine perfection a matter of an absolute infinity (primarily Spinoza and Hegel) vs. an infinity of kind, the issue of infinity as a Divine perfection really is the application of infinity to whatever primary qualities are assigned to God (e.g., power, will, love) as a way of contrasting them with the limited extent of the similar quality in man. What is commonly misunderstood, however, is that this does not at all mean that the quality applies absolutely without restrictions (the counterpart of the concept of an absolute infinity of kinds). It does mean, for example, that in the application of power God has no external or internal limitations due to deficiencies in His nature. One attribute of the Divine nature may limit another, but each attribute in its own right is infinite. There are always the traditional considerations of "what God cannot do," but these do not, as they do in man, spring originally from a state of inherent weakness.

The contrast of God as alone properly infinite becomes more striking in a view which sees the universe, and thus time and motion, as having had a definite beginning, and perhaps also a definite end. For here everything in the natural order is necessarily limited by the finite extent of time, and also by the limited life of the natural order and of everything within it. Oddly enough, this modern perspective has found itself more at home with actual infinities, at least in thought, whereas the classical view of the eternality of the world had a natural framework of infinity in extent of time but rejected it as a perfection. Of course, this reversal of an imperfection so that it becomes a perfection is understandable enough, since an eternal world could never become actual, whereas the modern conception of a beginning and an end to time and process fits perfectly into the classical concept of completion and actuality.

The classical rejection of the unlimited, and the consequent stress upon limitation as the vehicle of perfection, can hardly be over-stressed. Even Plato, who uses the unlimited and who nowhere rejects it as strongly as Aristotle does, is unequivocal in seeing limitation as the source of beauty, harmony, and thus of perfection. Later theologians meet this Platonic conservatism by asserting infinity of extent but preserving form as a mode of limitation, thus reconciling infinity with the classical notions of beauty and harmony as being dependent upon some limitation. What the new stress upon the actuality of infinity does is to remove some limitations but not all. The doctrine of an absolute infinity vs. an infinity of one kind, carries the metamorphosis of classical concepts a step further, but it is really in the contrast—and yet association—of infinity with unity that the radical break is made. Plato only hints at the transcendence of being by the Good; but Plotinus, and all who treat unity as a dominating concept in ontology, completes this revolution.

As was pointed out in discussing Plotinus and Hegel, although Plotinus "begins" systematically with the soul, he does so only in order to establish it as a mid-point, with greater diversity to be found in the body and in physical nature. The soul itself points to its contacts with realms characterized by an even greater unity. Such a hierarchical arrangement of modes of being according to degrees of unity is bound to end by transcending both being and thought in the One, as the source of both unity and the degrees of it present within being. Whenever the scheme of things is so ordered (infinity necessarily involving expansiveness), form and multiplicity are bound to fall and to be no longer characteristic of perfection at its ultimate.

Metaphysicians learned to deal with infinity, to rid it of its negative aspects, and, through infinity's association with form, to make is compatible with knowledge in its highest mode (though not with ordinary knowledge until the modern period). But unity as a guiding concept requires that the transcendence of form not be characteristic of the primal level, and thus infinity either again becomes disassociated from form and thus destructive to knowledge or is left behind with form on a secondary level of the hierarchy. The finite is to be contrasted with the infinite, but unity demands that such contrasts be transcended until the One becomes beyond either the finite or the infinite as the undivided source of both. Naturally thought fails here, for it is dependent upon distinctions and upon forms, and both of these are left behind in a definition of such a level of perfection.

Here the objections of Aristotle reappear, for it becomes obvious that scientific knowledge of such a source of being is impossible. The suggestion is fairly clear that even the ordinary "laws of thought" are suspended. Nothing in the One holds elements apart so that they may be grasped by the distinctions of thought. This is the meaning of Plotinus' description of the One as the source of all things without being itself any one thing. The One is the source of all beings but nothing is found in distinction from anything else, and hence no predication at all is possible. Distinctions, even the distinction of thought vs. its object, appear at a level lower than that which is fully perfect, i.e., fully one. It is not the chaos of Plato's receptacle, but it is indefiniteness of a kind. Here rationalism is lost, since the ultimate source of being, i.e., that which explains being, in its supreme unity must transcend that alone upon which reason can operate: distinctions and the diversity of definite objects.

One interesting point to note in considering the concepts of unity and infinity and their various applications to Divine perfection is that they form at least one basis for discussing the problem of evil. For instance, if, following the neo-Platonists, we use unity as the defining characteristic of perfection, then evil comes to be associated with multiplicity or the degree of distance from the Primal One. Such a view makes evil a matter of fact, a necessary consequence of the fullness of a creation that reaches to the farthest distance. This should cause us very little objection, nor is it a fault to be attributed to the source of being. Infinity, when associated with form, makes evil out to be lack of form (i.e., chaos) or the limitation implied in being finite. When, however, infinity is replaced by unity as the determining factor in perfection, then lack of particularity and distinction characterize perfection, and evil is the separation associated with individualization.

Even without completely analyzing evil in these terms, it is evident that *the determination of perfection is at the same time the specification of the nature of evil.* And since what constitutes perfection can vary, the same alternatives and flexibility characterize evil. In this sense the source of perfection must always be at the same time the ontological, although not necessarily the immediate, source of evil. The difficulty is not that of making the Divine creative source also the source of evil, for a deviation and thus a fall from its full perfection will always be necessitated in any creation. The problem is whether evil as such is contained within the Divine nature itself. It need not be, except as the Divine is the source of the created order and is the standard of perfection from which lesser beings of necessity deviate in varying degrees. In any case, the determination of Divine perfection must always be (by negation) at the same time the determination of the standard of evil.

Perhaps the most interesting argument for the necessity of infinity as primary in Divine perfection develops from the increasing attention given in modern thought to the variety of possible worlds as they are contrasted with our actualized natural order. This approach via the possibles become almost the distinctive characteristic of the modern metaphysician. Some hint of an order of possibles can be found in the concept of the "unlimited" in pre-Socratic thought, but this is almost always placed in contrast with what is perfect. The increasing positive attention which comes to be given to infinity as a possible perfection begins to bring with it increased attention to possible orders of nature. In classical thought there is little suggestion of any possible ontological framework other than our own. Medieval theologians (e.g., Aquinas), however, in finding it difficult to limit God's infinite thought to our order begin to postulate God's grasp in thought of a range of uncreated orders.

It is true that it was some time before it was possible to suggest any contingency (and thus freedom) in God's action in choosing from among the possible orders in His act of creation. The dominance of "actuality" in perfection (to be discussed below) acted as a restraining factor. But it is the increasing expansion of infinity (e.g. toward absolute infinity) that has supplied the greatest impetus toward giving serious consideration to "possibility" as a central concept for perfection. The revolution is completed when possibility finally comes to be a primary concept. Then all consideration begins (systematically speaking) by giving attention to the unlimited scope of possibility. This is particularly true when, as in Ockham, it is defined solely by the limit of self-contradiction. The radical changes which this requires in the concept of Divine perfection have their origin in the expansiveness introduced by the acceptance of infinity as primary.

Let us now take the terms "infinity" and "unity" and attempt a long range historical recapitulation of their metaphysical employment in the concept of Divine perfection. Infinity came to be a quality of perfection when it was dissociated from chaos and indeterminacy, and this was accomplished by making it compatible with form and, thus, with at least one mode of knowledge. Infinity then was subject to further expansion into an absolute infinity, an infinity of infinite kinds rather than just one mode of infinity. When this happens the natural world almost always comes to be viewed as merely one aspect of the Divine nature, so all-inclusive is such a concept of infinity. Even here knowledge is not necessarily transcended, since an infinite mode of knowledge is developed to parallel the ontological expansion. However, sometimes both the infinite and the finite are transcended in their opposition by placing what is Divinely perfect beyond both as the source of both. However, such a transcendence of infinity as applicable directly to Divine perfection usually only happens when unity comes to be the determining concept.

An absolute infinity has a kind of unity implied in its extent, such that nothing is conceivable beyond it. But in serious ontologies based upon unity as a primary concept such extreme multiplicity cannot be either ultimate or ultimately perfect. However, when unity receives such stress, then the earlier view of infinity tends to return, such that the First Principle is characterized by a multiplicity which is without definite structure or limit. As recognized classically, this raises what is fully perfect above the rational modes of knowing that are dependent upon form and distinction. An early rationalism rejected infinity on the grounds of its unknowability, but the assimilation of infinity with form eliminated this objection. For all ontologies which stress unity as primary in perfection, knowledge becomes directly applicable only at a secondary level. Perfection itself, when dominated by the concept of unity, is surrounded by a cloud of unknowing.

Infinities become commonplace in the late Middle Ages, and especially for the seventeenth-century rationalists. However, under the critical restraint of Kant, infinity once again was excluded as being disruptive of knowledge. Form and limitation again dominate, although this applies primarily to the phenomenal world. In Kant's noumenal realm hints of infinity return in the feeling of the sublime. What the understanding cannot know directly, aesthetic feeling may possibly experience indirectly. However, with Hegel infinity once again reigns supreme, while unity and its consequent unknowability recede into the background. The dialectical process, the development through opposition, the expression of Spirit in the unfolding of nature and history—all these combine to bring the Divine close to temporal multiplicity and to make it necessary for any God to be expansive to the ultimate degree in order to encompass all of this.

What, then, shall we do with "unity" and "infinity" in constructing a concept of Divine perfection? In a scheme in which possibles are given unlimited extent, a Divine nature must be absolutely infinite in intellect in order actually to comprehend this vast range, and if infinite in intellect then infinity must also apply to any nature possessing an intellect of this scope. Such being the case, unity can apply to Divine perfection not as its primary characteristic but as a consequence of the completely inclusive nature of the possibles when they are so liberally conceived. Knowledge would not be so much transcended by such an infinity, but only restricted in its grasp, i.e., unable to hold all such diverse possible individual entities simultaneously in attention. Since such a realm of possible entities, and the intellect infinitely applicable to them, would form only a part of the Divine nature, such a God would transcend even absolute infinity (and thus knowledge) by possessing a nature of which an absolute infinity of possibles would be only one aspect.

9

FORM

AND

TRANSCENDENCE

As should be clear from the previous discussion, the issue of form vs. transcendence is really dependent upon a prior consideration. For instance, if, as for Aristotle, what is perfect must be (at least in principle) fully knowable, then form will always represent perfection. If infinity violates form, as it does in Aristotle's early formulation, then infinity must be excluded as a Divine perfection, whether or not it is allowed existence in some other manner. When the conception of infinity can be transformed to be made compatible with form by being made fully actual, then it can be accepted as a characteristic of perfection. On the other hand, whenever unity is a key ontological concept, then form will come to represent distinction and must be transcended. In this case discursive knowledge is also transcended, so that knowability and form no longer represent perfection. Now transcendence of the bonds of being, of form and infinity, is more in keeping with perfection than is rational grasp. Such perfection may still be knowable, but only by means of a more immediate vision than rational discourse and only after a difficult process designed to break the bonds which form imposes.

Intelligibility, which means primarily amenability to form, is Aristotle's guiding concept, and this is never totally reversed where Divine perfection is concerned. As different conceptions of intelligibility are framed, Aristotle's more strict requirements are abandoned. It is never asserted that God is unintelligible, although His transcendence of form, distinction, and ordinary logical grasp will often make the Divine nature appear unknowable simply by contrast. Whenever Aristotle's restrictions of completion, definiteness, and limit are set aside for Divinity, then knowledge is bound to become more difficult and probably will require an indirect approach. Although "knowledge" will become a different kind of thing from plain discourse about the ordinary levels of being, it is never set aside completely. Standards of intelligibility vary; and, where transcendence of the limits of being is involved, these become debatable. Differences about the knowability of a perfect Being represent not an argument of knowability vs. unknowability but basic disagreement over ontological structure and the nature of its ultimate source.

Exemption from motion is perhaps the most debatable characteristic of perfection which both Plato and Aristotle insist upon. Form again represents completion and thus lack of motion, but this is no difficulty for Plato and Aristotle since they are able to trace motion to ontological sources other than what is perfect. When, however, there is to be only one first principle in ontology then no one can agree completely with the classical exclusion of motion from perfection. All metaphysical thought after Plotinus accounts for being by means of a single first principle and accepts motion into Divinity in some sense; the question is, in what sense. Motion for Aristotle meant change and incompleteness. Just as infinity was altered to transform it from imperfection to perfection, so now motion is altered in concept so that Divinity itself may be the source of motion but still be itself unchanging and complete in nature. Motion in

Divinity gives life and power to all created by it. Motion in creatures represents life and power also, but it is imperfect here in its involvement with incompleteness and the possibility of a radical change in nature.

When we consider Plato's use of beauty as evidence for, or as a reflection of, the presence of perfection, then Plato's use of form and motionlessness in defining perfection is somewhat altered. Beauty for Plato is usually connected with the presence of form, but form itself is subject to some transcendence as it is not for Aristotle. Although it transcends the natural world, form does not transcend the structure of either being or reason, since it is itself the very embodiment of these two characteristics. However, Plato's concept of the Good has aspects which transcend both being and reason, and the Good is surely associated with the source of beauty. Thus, in Platonism is to be found a basis for the development of a concept of Divine perfection which transcends being, although it is probable that for Plato the Good is simply a higher form and does not transcend form altogether. Beauty, whenever it becomes an avenue to, or is used as evidence for, the nature of Divine perfection, almost always involves a transcendence of at least the ordinary structures of knowing. Beauty is more akin to what is immediately grasped than that which requires discourse and distinction, so it is not surprising that Plotinus' second term for the One is often the Good.

An important point to note here in connection with transcendence and perfection is that the Greek and Hellenistic conceptions usually apply the same concept of perfection to both gods and men, although the Divine always embodies perfection more fully. As extreme transcendence comes to characterize perfection, Divine perfection tends to develop special characteristics and human nature and the natural order have opposite, or at least quite different, characteristics (e.g., infinite vs. finite). Whatever transcendent aspects can be found in Plato and Plotinus, their First Principles each share their characteristics with men. Later on, God comes to have a nature and a life quite His own; His perfection now makes Him unique. This involves transcendence of a more drastic kind and, since natural categories no longer fit, problems of knowledge become more serious to handle. Perfection, which once gods and men shared however unequally, comes to be the very quality which separates Divinity from man.

It is the transcendence of form, as in Dionysius and Plotinus, which makes the use of language so difficult and the grasp of knowledge so insecure. Whenever perfection means the transcendence of the structure of being, our language (which is derived from being's qualities) becomes faulty and at times misleading. When unity's demands are so strong that the law of identity is suspended whenever the One is characterized, our language, being dependent upon structure and distinctions, is robbed of its power to describe. As long as form is preserved, even if it is the Platonic form which transcends nature, language has an applicability. Whenever perfection requires the transcendence of form, as it does for Plotinus, Dionysius, and the mystics, language and its usefulness become a serious and primary problem. Concepts may still lead us to perfection, but now they can never describe its nature, except by negation and indirection. Those who preserve form as ultimately characteristic of Divine perfection, suffer less over language and its inadequacies, since rational discourse remains applicable here without fear of distortion.

Nevertheless, the primary asset of such extreme transcendence of form is that it places Divinity beyond any question of dependence upon any being other than itself. Such transcendence is usually arrived at through the attempt to rid God of His dependence upon the structure of being, which is necessary whenever there is a similarity in nature between God and being in general. If both God and nature are apprehended by the use of the same concepts, then there is always the danger that Divinity will become subjected to those structures and thus be as dependent upon them as are men. In this way the transcendence of form is dependent upon the concept of self-sufficiency (see below), just as, in another respect, form and transcendence are determined by the considerations of infinity and unity. Infinity need not now cause Divine perfection to transcend form, but unity as a primary attribute usually does. Similarly, the desire to protect the Divine self-sufficiency often requires that form and the structures of being both be passed beyond.

Except within the mystical tradition, metaphysics and theology have hardly, since the time of Plotinus and Dionysius, known a view which stresses the ultimate transcendence of form and of all ordinary modes of knowledge. Augustine and Anselm are aware of aspects of transcendence, but Divine perfection seems to be fully within the limits of form and thus to pose no insuperable problems of knowledge. Already Divine perfection is being moved out into categories which will make it distinct in kind from the characteristics which describe man, but the rational bonds which hold man and God together are, although loosened, never broken. Aquinas assimilates infinity to form, and Ockham makes our knowledge of God less direct and less subject to definitive formulation, but all that Ockham speaks about is fully within the framework required for rational discourse.

Spinoza and Hegel, of course, represent the extreme optimism of reason. The concept of the Divine nature is infinitely expanded by them, but so also is man's rational grasp. These two natures may be somewhat different, but both God and man reason essentially alike if man's reason is properly trained. Man is as capable of simultaneous grasp as is God, and there is nothing beyond form and no form to which reason does not extend. Kant's metaphysical skepticism limits known form to the form of man's understanding, but at the same time every aspect of the phenomenal world is within this grasp. It is possible that God Himself might transcend form on Kant's view, but it is not possible for reason to know this directly with any assurance. With Hegel all restrictions are removed from reason. In a classical view, reason derived knowledge from only a limited group of objects; for Hegel reason must now encompass an infinite variety of historical and metaphysical data and is considered ideally suited to this arduous task.

Form, then, is transcended in Hegelian conceptions of Divine perfection in the sense that form is not sufficient for perfection but must be combined with passion, with the material process of the world and all of its individual aspects. Just as unity transcends form in moving perfection above the structures of being, so Hegel transcends form by moving downward to include an infinite variety of material and historical phenomena. However, form still remains in all cases central to the doctrine of perfection. In some theories it is the very epitome of perfection, both Divine and human. In others it points the way upward beyond its own necessarily distinct existence toward an even higher level. For still others, form must be opposed to the historical and material particularity of the world process and perfection attained only in the dialectical process expressed and consummated by this opposition.

Just as form always plays a central, if somewhat varying, role in any concept of Divine perfection, so also is there always some degree of transcendence present. Even if the mode of perfection is the same for men and gods, the Divine still transcends the natural realm by embodying the characteristics of perfection more fully. When the preservation of self-sufficiency in Divinity demands that it be placed beyond the necessarily multiple framework of being, extreme transcendence is introduced, with all its consequent problems of the adequacy of language and the development of a unique mode of knowing. When Divinity can only be found in the total process, as with either Spinoza or Hegel, the transcendence of every particular aspect of nature is implied, even though the perfection of the Divine life does not transcend a reason of infinitely subtle power and range.

10

ACTUALITY

AND

SELF-SUFFICIENCY

The thought of Divine perfection often turns the mind to the concept of "actuality." Nothing could be clearer in Aristotle than his characterization of perfection primarily in terms of actuality. That which is fully actual is form, free from matter, motion, and change. These latter three characteristics are excluded from perfection not so much on their own grounds as on the ground that each implies a lack of actuality. Obviously, it is primarily actuality that is important to perfection. Matter, motion, and change may be included in Divinity if it can be shown that they do not damage the Divine actuality, as Aristotle held they would. Spinoza made matter compatible with perfection by making it fully amenable to an infinite reason. Aristotle's reason was more limited and could not assimilate matter without damage to its ability to achieve completion.

Behind actuality (which after Aristotle meant excluding matter, motion, and change until someone could free them from the charge of subversion) lies a concept even more important to perfection, i.e., self-sufficiency. For actuality is crucial only because it indicates a lack of dependence upon anything outside of itself; anything not fully actual runs the risk of standing in need of something other than itself to complete its nature. Thus, as the concept of perfection developed, even full actuality could be taken away from perfection and the theory might still fit the classical pattern, if only a way could be found to protect the complete self-sufficiency of the Divine. What is fully actual is surely self-sufficient. What is not fully actual, or what involves matter, motion, or change, may be self-sufficient; but the risk and the burden of proof fall upon the proposer of the innovation.

Speaking of the unmoved mover, Aristotle asserts contemplation to be the most self-sufficient activity (*Metaphysics,* 1074 b 34 and *Nich. Ethics,* 1178 b 21). This indicates the governing power which self-sufficiency as a concept has. Contemplation may be ascribed to Aristotle's principle of perfection because contemplation is the best evidence that can be given of self-sufficiency. It is also clear that activity is not, as many believe, incompatible in this case with perfection, although it may be in a theory that stresses the dominance of unity. What is fully perfect may act, but its action must be the kind that testifies to its self-sufficiency, whereas our imperfect motions testify so clearly to our dependent status. Not all motion is incompatible with perfection for Aristotle, but it must be a motion of only a certain type, i.e., motion which seeks nothing outside of its own nature.

Certain kinds of motion and activity are compatible with perfection, and even the Aristotelian framework could be modified to allow matter, motion, and change as long as self-sufficiency could be maintained. All patterns of perfection, however, are not this generous. Plotinus forces the One to transcend all such attribution, since the complete transcendence of normal categories is itself perhaps the best way to insure the Divine self-sufficiency. If it transcends all particular attribution, then it cannot be made dependent upon them. This is the reason why so many later theologies make the fundamental split in all things to be: that-which-is-the-cause-of-itself vs. that-which-has-its-cause-in-another. The outcome of this is to draw a radical contrast between Divinity, dependent for its existence upon nothing outside of itself, and all of being and its particular beings, whose primary characteristic is their need for other beings or for other parts of the structure of being.

Here is the real unity of the whole theological and metaphysical tradition: what distinguishes Divinity is its perfection, and fundamentally this means its self-sufficiency, its dependence upon nothing other than itself for its own existence and activity. Classically this has been conceived in terms of actuality, and usually full actuality, but this can be and has been altered when other ways are found to preserve the Divine self-sufficiency, whether such a nature voluntarily involves itself with other beings or not. If infinity did not threaten the unmoved mover's self-sufficiency, it could be ascribed to it as an attribute. But as Aristotle thought of infinity, it meant the denial of actuality and thus could not even be considered as an attribute of what was perfect.

When Spinoza literally identifies reality and perfection, yet another solution becomes possible. All of matter, motion, and change are now included within Divine perfection, but absolute infinity is also here, so that the intellect is able to grasp everything *qua* actualized. For Aristotle and Plato matter, motion, and change all stood as an impediment to knowledge and thus could not be included in perfection because they introduced obscurities. With a more powerful theory of knowledge, one which is able to encompass even an absolute infinity, perfection may include all of reality, now that it can be adequately understood. Such understanding for Spinoza banishes contingency, so that actuality is still a hallmark of perfection when all of reality is viewed properly. Lack of actuality indicates only a lack of improved understanding. All aspects of reality are included in Divine perfection, but only when they are grasped by an understanding strengthened to the point of grasping absolute infinity. All aspects of reality appear, but they appear as actualized.

A more difficult problem develops with the beginning of a stress upon possible and unrealized entities within the Divine understanding. When Aquinas introduces never-to-be-actualized-worlds into God's intellect, actuality as a necessary characteristic of perfection takes on an altered meaning. God is no longer fully actual in the sense that every possible concept will eventually come to have existence in concrete reality. He can remain fully actual in nature quite easily, even if the unrealized possibles in themselves remain only possible, if His actualization of them in any other way is not really possible. This is the solution which Leibniz and Thomas choose, although both Spinoza and Hegel deny the unrealized actuality of any possible entity, making God and the natural world quite close in nature. Whenever unrealized possibles appear, actuality as a perfection can be preserved, but it can never be the simple actuality of the Aristotelian scheme.

The issue, of course, hinges on the presence (or lack of it) of contradiction within the nature of the possibles as individual entities. If, as Leibniz thought, all are not compossible, then they cannot all be actualized as Spinoza asserted. Since Hegel's scheme requires clash and opposition for its very development, the actualization of incompatible possibles is more easily accomplished within such a dialectical framework. However, if we begin with the very generous definition of "possible" which Ockham gives (i.e., any conceivable entity is a possible if its essential definition involves no internal self-contradiction), then the realm of possible individual entities is so indefinitely multiplied that not even Hegel's gigantic process can accommodate them all. Full actuality cannot easily be attributed to a Divinity whose intellect encompasses such diversity, and the maintenance of some form of actuality, and also of the perfection of self-sufficiency, now depends upon the adequacy of the account we give of God's mode of choice for actualization from among these ultimately incompatible possible entities.

When possible individuals are so liberally expanded that the concrete world obviously could not accommodate them all, then the nature of "argument" is also somewhat changed. All arguments become merely possible, and what is true with certainty can only mean what must be the case even if our particular world should not exist. All other truths and all other arguments are contingent, containing at best a degree of probability, which is derived in turn from the degree of probability possessed by the possible entities to which the argument refers. Here actuality as a Divine perfection can only mean the ability of the Divine to accomplish the actualization of one basic structure of being, which He constitutes from among the possible individual entities. Self-sufficiency can only mean God's ability to contain all of the absolutely infinite possibles within the Divine nature and to actualize a living and a self-sustaining natural order from among this vast range, giving it independence from Divinity but subject to His ultimate control.

During the entire history of theology, even when actuality has been variously conceived, self-sufficiency has always been maintained as central to the very nature of Divinity's perfection and as that which distinguishes it from all else. In this respect much nonsense has been written about the Platonic Forms as a model of perfection. They do represent *one* type of perfection for Plato, but Plato has no single first principle. Even a cursory reading of the *Phaedrus* will show the kind of perfection which "soul" represents in Platonic thought. As the cause of its own motion, the soul exhibits a mode of perfection which becomes increasingly important for Plato and which becomes central for the neo-Platonists. Both Plato and Aristotle distinguish various types of motion, and by no means do all types represent defect. Interestingly enough, it is easier to see the rational motion of soul as perfect within Platonism than it is to view such motion as perfect in Aristotle, although probably it is to be found in the circular or rotary motion of some of the heavenly spheres.

It is not so much a negative attitude toward motion as it is a positive attitude toward actuality which guides Aristotle, so that if the motion were of a kind that is compatible with actuality it could be acceptable. Motion often is an evidence of imperfection in the object, indicating a lack or a deficiency, and such motion must be rejected as representing an imperfect state. For Plato self-sufficiency is more important than actuality, so that the activity of soul (or at least its ideal rational activity) is more easily acceptable as perfect, since as found an ideal model it is not inconsistent with self-sufficiency. The difficulty comes with later Platonism, committed to a single First Principle, since it must find a way to combine in one source the perfection represented by motionless form with that represented by the actuality of a rational and self-sustaining soul.

All serious theologians have allowed at least some motion to be compatible with perfection, although the type of motion is highly restricted by some and made more inclusive by others, e.g., Aristotle and Aquinas vs. Spinoza and Hegel. Anyone who constructs an ontology around a single First Principle must make it as least the *source* of motion, even if God does not actually exhibit certain kinds of motion Himself. If the universe is eternal, as it is for Plotinus, then the problem is easier, for there need be no beginning creative activity. Constant and eternal emanation of the lower orders from the higher can present motion as continually produced by the One without making the One itself contain internal motion. However, if once there was nothing and creative activity brought time into existence, some activity has to be predicated of the source of this present structure of being.

Whatever the type of motion and whatever the intimacy of its presence in an ontological First Principle, this involves no problem as long as the Divine self-sufficiency is maintained. Not such unanimous agreement can be found concerning full actuality. To some it seems necessary, but for these metaphysicians the First Principle is seldom the single principle ontologically responsible for creation (e.g., Aristotle.) If modes of possibility are to be found in God, as the later medievalists find them, then no harm comes to perfection as long as this is not such as to damage the Divine self-sufficiency. The alternative here, if self-sufficiency is destroyed, is to return to ultimately plural first principles, since only a self-sufficient principle can be the single and prior source of all being. If He is to create and to be responsible for creative sustenance, His own ability to control and sustain Himself cannot itself be in question.

Here again the attractions are obvious if we make Divine perfection a matter of extreme transcendence. What transcends the structures of being, what lies beyond and is not bound even by our laws of thought, cannot itself be in jeopardy of being compromised or subjected to the contingencies of existence. Plotinus sees the necessity for protecting the self-sufficiency of the One by its transcendence of all structures, and Aquinas accepts this in a modified form when he makes God capable of affecting the world but incapable of being affected by it. This is the traditional neo-Platonic emanation theory in which power flows only outward and downward, and the upward reach is accomplished only by abandoning in turn each lower nature, so that what finally touches God is only a part of God Himself. This inability to be affected by the temporal events of the natural order is Aquinas' own way of insuring the Divine self-sufficiency in the face of the greater amount of activity and motion and involvement Thomas must ascribe to his God.

Although all motion becomes a part of the Divine nature for both Spinoza and Hegel, self-sufficiency is preserved through the traditional concept of actuality. That is, the total process will eventually become, and may always be viewed as, fully actualized. Even an extreme variety of motion does not introduce difficulties into Divinity as long as we follow the conservative avenue of achieving self-sufficiency (i.e., full actuality). Leibniz essentially follows this alternative too. His God moves as human souls do, but no abandonment of traditional perfection is involved since the whole process will be fully actualized according to pre-established harmony. The choice among possibles and the ultimate non-actuality of some, all this is part of a necessary process which allows for no alternatives. Plato did not give necessity much prominence; but since the time of Aristotle, necessity has always been a means of assuring self-sufficiency, even in the face of a lack of the full actualization of all possibles.

When any freedom of choice or any contingency is introduced into the Divine activity, then preserving the perfection of self-sufficiency becomes a not impossible but at least a more difficult task. Freedom lifts the bonds of necessity from the Divine activity, and necessity has always been the great preserver of self-sufficiency. Not a few theologians (e.g., Augustine) have been induced to bind God's action (and thus also man's) by necessity, for thereby no question is raised about God's self-sufficiency or His ability to create unopposed and to retain full control over His creation as well as Himself. This accounts for the resistance found within the tradition to placing any contingency within the Divine nature. The introduction of motion, as has been indicated, is not a particular difficulty; but the possibility of loss of self-sufficiency is difficult to guard against, and necessity is always a sure guarantee and a powerful guardian.

The introduction of a range of unrealized possibles into the Divine knowledge requires that God's basis for decision be accounted for. Aquinas and Leibniz do this, but they simply make the criteria for selection themselves necessary and capable of yielding only one decision. When, however, the voluntarism of either a Scotus or an Ockham enters, the situation is more complicated. Now genuine alternatives must be allowed, although choice is never without a rational ground in Divinity. In such a situation it is more difficult to preserve the full control (and self-control) of Divinity while still preserving genuine alternatives in His activity of selection. Actuality and necessity, the traditional means for accomplishing this, are now ruled out, and new ways must be found to reach the classical goal of self-sufficiency. Without this quality, no First Principle is able from Himself alone to account for creation or to be assured of continued or at least eventual control. There may be some today who simply prefer not to construct a theory of the Divine nature; but, if we do, it probably should include the more modern notions of freedom, while at the same time preserving the classical distinction between Divinity and humanity, i.e., His full self-sufficiency. Such an attempt will be made when freedom is discussed.

11

POWER

AND

MOTION

Embracing perfection within the bonds of necessity is perhaps the clearest and most obvious way to protect the Divine self-sufficiency. Whenever the stress upon unrealized possibles makes such a controlling necessity impossible, then one way of preserving the Divine self-sufficiency (religiously expressed as "omnipotence") is through an increased stress upon "power" as a central attribute. Power may be a limited force as long as necessity controls (e.g., Aristotle), or it may receive slightly increased stress (e.g., Plato) even without necessity's full control, if perfection resides partly in another area (i.e., the Forms) and if power is at least sufficient to accomplish its creative task. When power as a Divine attribute receives stress, motion seems necessarily involved in the control and in the operation of that power. Our natural power is often not sufficient to provide us with the control which we find necessary to preserve ourselves. Thus the Divine power must be infinite if it is to be thought of as perfect, particularly if the possible entities in the Divine intellect are postulated as absolutely infinite. From the extension of possibility to an absolute infinity of possible entities, we derive the need for a perfect power to be itself infinite if it is to be able to exercise the requisite control.

For Plato power means rational control, and this is the soul's central characteristic. Soul always requires an involvement with motion (in fact, it is the ultimate source of motion), but this is no denial of perfection for a Platonist who idealizes the soul. Irrational and chaotic motion is a violation of perfection, but Plato attributes such motion to another source. A neo-Platonist would predicate (of his First Principle) neither rational motion nor irrational motion nor rest, but the One will be the unseparated source of all while yet transcending these distinctions. When Plato later (in the *Sophist*, 247E) defines being as power, a new possibility is opened and power may be treated as perfection itself, expressed in a variety of modes with varying degrees of perfection. With a view of the identity of power and being (which Plato himself never develops), "soul" and "form" can be reconciled, and motion need no longer be considered necessarily characteristic only of a lower order.

Plato links power to stability of nature and to the lack of radical change in characteristics, both of which are central to Divinity. Sufficient power secures control, so that only that motion which indicates a lack or a loss of control need be considered imperfect. In a Platonic scheme power must be rationally directed and oriented toward the Good in order to be perfect, but the action and consequent motion of such a power only indicate its perfection. The patterns (i.e., the Forms) which guide such power do not themselves change, but the motion which is in accord with them is the very expression of perfection. Plato's possible Forms are not infinite, so his principle of power (i.e., soul) need not be infinite in order to operate effectively. Contrary to much prejudice, it is actually in Platonism, and its later development in neo-Platonisms, that the main example of motion as perfection is to be found. Aristotle offers a more limited example, but even he allows some types of activity and motion to be expressions of perfection.

Development, motion, and seeking tend for Aristotle to imply the lack of an attained end, but we must not take this as casting an aspersion upon all motion. What we must inquire about is whether motion indicates the presence of an imperfection, as it so often does, or whether it represents instead the activity characteristic of Divinity. Power cannot be power without involving motion; but, if the power is sufficient for the accomplishment of its objective, then it can only be a limited perspective which would consider such motion an imperfection. The majority of human motions do indicate lack and need, and their success or failure is a matter of contingency. Divinity is not restricted by its perfection from any activity it wishes to accomplish, but such action cannot arise from lack or need. It must be the expression of its superabundance of power (perhaps however only brought to expression by an excess of love).

It is primarily from Aristotle, and not from Plato, that the attribute of rest receives its stress as a perfection. Aristotle prefers rest because he associates motion with time, change, and incompleteness. It is these three which are the questionable qualities, and rest is an important Divine attribute only as it stands for their opposite. No God can be subject to time in the sense in which we are, otherwise He could not be its creator. Change outside our control is essentially what describes our nature, and it is primarily this which cannot be ascribed to God. Our change is never perfectly within our control and is always subject to a radical form, i.e., passing away. Divinity may be subject to change, provided that its power is perfect and yields full control and that its nature cannot pass away. Incompleteness is not even incompatible with Divinity if it is the incompleteness of any given, temporal moment. However, our lives and all of nature are subject to ultimate cessation without completion, and a possibility of this kind will always remain incompatible with perfection. It is easy enough to deny any of the classical restrictions required by perfection, but it is very difficult to show that such an "imperfect

God" is sufficiently able to perform the functions required of Him (e.g., creation or salvation).

Matter for Aristotle was incompatible with perfection, since it represented potentiality and thus the impetus to motion. Time is also a consequence of motion for Aristotle. Although this associates time principally with physical nature, it does not necessarily make it in every aspect incompatible with Divinity. If any motion were found consistent with Divinity's nature, Aristotle would find a form of time associated with it. His motion and form of life being different, God as the creator of all natural motion (and thus of time) cannot be subject to either motion or time in the same way that we are, but Augustine's discussion of time in the *Confessions* is an excellent example of the way in which a form of time may legitimately be ascribed to God.

Plotinus can allow no motion or division to be within the One, although it is the source of these without itself exhibiting their qualities in distinction. This indicates the sense in which, whenever we deal with a single First Principle, any aspect of the natural world whatsoever must be ascribed to God as its source. It is a simple enough doctrine that an effect need not exist in its cause in the same way in which it comes to exist after gaining the independence of coming-into-being. At least in this sense of ultimate source, every quality or aspect of any entity within the natural order must be traced back to God as ultimate cause. Otherwise we either do not have a single First Principle or else it does not serve its rational explanatory function, which it must be able to do if it was able to effect and sustain creation in the beginning. This need not involve a doctrine of predestination, nor must it remove contingent responsibility from men. But it does set us the difficult task of reconciling (with the Divine nature itself) every predicate that is possible within the natural order, however differently such qualities may exist in a transcendent and perfect Divinity.

Any theology which stresses infinite possible entities and a Divine actualizing *will* must give a primary position to *power* as a perfection. "Will" is nothing but the control of power as it actualizes in accord with one (but not the only possible) standard of value. God becomes responsible for His choice and for the potentialities of good and evil present within His elected structure of being, but He is not necessarily responsible for every contingent choice of man. God's motion in the activity of selecting at the moment of creation represents not imperfection, but the operation of His infinite, and hence perfect, power. Such motion internal to the Divine nature, resulting in the constitution of a natural order outside of it, represents the basis within Divinity for the natural sequence of time. Here the exercise of power is an evidence of the basic perfection required of a Divinity, i.e., its self-sufficiency. God's power remains fully actual in its applicability, even if vast numbers of possible individual entities necessarily remain as potential within His nature. His absolutely infinite power retains ultimate control; He is perfect.

12

SIMPLICITY

AND

DIVISION

It is interesting to note that the usual formulation of the famed "Ockham's razor" (entities must not be multiplied without necessity) does not seem to appear in Ockham's writings. Rather, he often uses a form of the traditional maxim: plurality is not to be posited without necessity (see *Reportatio* II, qu. 150). The metaphysician will immediately recognize this as simply the usual theological goal of preserving a simplicity of basic ontological structure. Infinity was rejected by Aristotle partly on the grounds that its indefinite multiplicity would destroy the simplicity necessary for his theory of knowledge. As the powers of reason become expanded, the urgency to reject infinity was reversed, since if infinity is brought within reason's control it no longer violates either the simplicity necessary for ontological structure or for knowledge. Plotinus is often considered the prime advocate of simplicity in a First Principle, but

Ockham's use of the traditional phrase indicates how widely recognized is the norm of simplicity among theologians.

Simplicity ought not to be confused with unity. Actually unity is only one way of achieving the goal of simplicity which can be reached through the use of other concepts (i.e., form). Simplicity, then, is an important concept, perhaps second in importance only to self-sufficiency, but it is a relative term. That is, ontologists have provided for it through the use of various concepts, all the way from Plotinus and absolute unity to Spinoza and absolute infinity. There is no one avenue, then, which a modern ontologist needs to follow, nor need he reject the desirability of simplicity as a primary characteristic for a First Principle simply because he objects to one historical way in which this has been achieved. Contemporary interest in theology may be pursued, but the modern ontologist must either satisfy the requirement of simplicity in his basic structure or demonstrate that this classical requirement may be set aside without disastrous consequences (e.g., paralyzing division). Simplicity as a concept, of course, is not an end in itself; it is a primary concept (i.e., a norm) for theologians because of the desirable consequences of its presence in Divinity and the difficult problems which appear in its absence.

Simplicity, therefore, is a desirable characteristic primarily because *it prevents division*. Some theologians allow distinctions to remain present within the Divine nature, whereas some do not; all theologians exclude division. If self-sufficiency has been shown to be the chief, if not the only, basis for making a radical distinction between God and man, division also serves as a crucial and basic means to separate the First Principle from all that follows after it. Every created thing is capable of division. Such a capacity is helpful in allowing us to deal with multiplicity as we must do, and it makes possible the removal from us at times of undesirable parts. But this beneficial characteristic is capable of being carried to extremes, until our very nature is divided against itself, paralyzing action and often resulting in destruction or even in the loss of our nature (e.g., schizophrenia). Such a ground for division, present within the very structure itself, cannot be characteristic of Divinity, although nothing could be more indicative of human nature. We can be destroyed and can destroy because of our potentially divisible nature, and the natural world is such that it allows this division to take place. In Divinity the presence of simplicity makes that nature basically different, i.e., not subject to these faults.

What makes a God "Divine" is his immunity to the internal grounds for destruction always present within man and nature. This does not at all mean that Divine perfection is not the source for every quality and characteristic found within the natural order; it must be so, or else there cannot be a single First Principle. On the other hand, God cannot be the source for and the creator of the realm of nature unless He exists in some mode that gives Him creative power sufficient to this awesome task. The Divine nature possesses every natural trait, but He does so in such a way that these are held together and their divisive or destructive powers are neutralized; simplicity accomplishes this crucial task. The presence of simplicity in a controlling fashion, sometimes sought for by men but seldom achieved, makes possible the presence of an absolute infinity of entities (some realized and some not) without the least fear of causing a division within the Divine nature.

Simplicity also has a logical or epistemological role which requires that it be made central to any description of Divinity. The purpose of constructing a metaphysical First Principle is to explain the multiple and perhaps conflicting phenomena which seem too great in variety and extent to explain themselves. This is not a scientific explanation, although the process is similar to that of reference to a theory or law; but "God" does explain by serving as a point to which *all* phenomena may be referred as to their source, whether directly or indirectly. No explanation results if the phenomena and the First Principle both exist either in the same mode or with equal multiplicity. "Explanation" takes place when natural phenomena come to be seen as pre-existing in a different and in a higher mode, as in a source which itself requires no further reference. And it is the quality of simplicity which makes the First Principle higher in mode of existence (i.e., Divine) and renders further tracing of causes unnecessary. A restless intellect in search of causes can only be satisfied and come to rest in this way. Simplicity alone explains.

The way in which simplicity is achieved (and with it a resolution of the intellect's restlessness) varies in each classical metaphysic, but simplicity can always be found operating either explicitly or implicitly. It is the hallmark of those thinkers whose writings have been preserved out of the too vast store of man's written word. Their thought has managed to embody this principle, to give simplicity to their multiple thoughts. The distinctive characteristic of all "classical" metaphysics is that within a given constructed intellectual framework it is possible to reduce the great multiplicity of life and/or nature to a few (if not a single) central concepts in terms of which much is brought into intellectual resolution, i.e., explanation. Many important metaphysical writings are an absolute maze of sentences and sometimes baffling concepts, but beneath this surface men have time and again made the discovery of an essential simplicity of First Principles and of explanation made possible by referring a great deal to a few concepts. This quality distinguishes the writer who becomes "classical" from his equally subtle and perhaps profound contemporary. The simplicity of formal style and analysis demanded by so many moderns is but the surface and thus superficial counterpart of this basic or underlying simplicity of First Principles which is the mark of the clear philosophical intellect.

At first glance Plato's preference for the principle of "mixture" (primarily in the *Philebus*) might seem to go against the supposed requirement of simplicity. Actually, what Plato's preference for "mixture" indicates is the variety of ways in which a simplicity of ontological principles can be maintained. Plato's basic principles are about three in number in the *Timaeus,* which indicates Plato's ultimate plurality of principles, but this certainly evidences some degree of simplicity of structure at the same time. In the *Philebus* he will allow no unmixed life to be the ideal, but the principles which guide mixture (the Good, harmony, etc.) indicate that this strictly controlled process (i.e., mixing the elements which we allow to enter into our lives) is itself one effective way of achieving simplicity. Harmony guides mixture and is surely itself another form of simplicity. At the end of the *Philebus* the Good cannot be described by one idea but must be pursued by three. Unity is given second place in importance for a mixture that is controlled by the Good, which is neither indefinitely multiple nor absolutely one in concept; but simplicity remains the goal even when harmony rather than unity is its means.

Perhaps most characteristic of both Spinoza and Plotinus is the ultimate duality of metaphysical viewpoint which is always present in their writing. Within the structure constructed by both men any aspect may be viewed in two ways (e.g., in time or under eternity; looking toward the One or looking away from it). However, it is also true that both men give an unquestioned preference to one perspective over the other, although both viewpoints remain ultimately possible. "Under eternity" and "toward the One" are to be preferred because of the contrasting simplicity which they yield. The intellect finds under the preferred perspective a reduction of multiplicity, a simplicity of conceptual framework and the opposite of the tendency toward division which the second and more common perspective represents. The conversion of the intellect is to a new perspective which yields simplicity precisely because it comprehends multiple phenomena and a variety of modes of existence in terms of a causal source whose own structure is, if not absolutely simple, at least less complex in structure.

Philosophers have always tended to label as "mystical" any view which requires that rational discourse at any point be set aside. However, the more responsible representatives of such a transcendental tendency have always been quite clear and detailed as to the reasons why such a "passing beyond" is necessary. Such writers are quite rational and articulate in pointing out their reasons for considering that rational discourse becomes inadequate at certain crucial points. Plotinus sees that reason necessarily depends upon distinction, and it is not a reckless anti-rationalism which makes him go on to place the exact nature of the One above rational discourse; it is his desire to insure simplicity. Plotinus is a good representative of those writers who are aware of the defects in the natural order that flow from the possibility of division and its dependence upon the multiplicity inherent in distinctions. Others, such men claim, represent the Divine nature as possessing all too many of the same flaws inherent in the natural order. Simplicity is the perfection which distinguishes God from men, and Plotinus is a rigorist who sees this as demanding the denial of even the distinctions necessary for logical and rational structure. All structures and entities are present within the One, but present as in a cause and under a mode of absolute simplicity which makes rational structure not applicable at this level. Reason is operative beginning only on a secondary level where distinctions begin to appear in sharp contrast.

On the other hand, Ockham is a thinker who never relaxes rational structure, and the result is that for him only a complex concept of God is possible. The best we can do is to sort out the attributes we feel to be necessary to Divinity, but the concept we construct can never be such as to exhibit the ultimate reconciliation of these attributes with one another. Language depends upon clear distinctions and so yields at best a concept still complex, whereas perfection strives for simplicity in Divinity. Here Ockham grasps the reason for the unsatisfactory feeling we have about even the best descriptions of the Divine nature. The language in which these must be stated requires a more complex structure than we feel able to attribute to God Himself. This is the basic incongruity which all theologians have struggled with: the commensurability of a complex language structure with the natural order but not with the simplicity necessary to Divine perfection.

What we can do with language we must do, since the meaning of theology requires that we speak. For example, the "ontological argument" is a means of bringing the mind to an awareness of the problems involved in the basic inadequacy of concepts that are of necessity based upon a complexity characteristic of the natural order. We construct a complex concept of Divinity, achieving as much simplicity of structure as possible, and then perhaps proceed via the negative method to deny the appropriateness of the aspects that are inadequate because of the complexity necessary in conceptual form. However, such a problem becomes most extreme for those theologians who stress the priority of unity as perhaps the most nearly adequate term for Divinity. Simplicity, as has been shown, can be achieved through less severe means, and the modern tendency has been to find a more basic complexity in Divinity and then to find divine attributes powerful enough to encompass this and to provide for simplicity through control. Leibniz' discussion of the possibles and the compossibles illustrates this more modern problem.

In any view where unity is stressed, such as Plotinus', there cannot be either unrealized possibles in the First Principle or possible individual entities which are not compossible. For unrealized possibles require at least one ultimate distinction, i.e., between those which are actualized and those which are not. Often such a situation calls for a decision to be made by the First Principle, an activity of which the Plotinian One is incapable. Even more serious is the presence within one framework of possible entities which are not all compossible, particularly if the criteria for selection are not absolutely binding (as they are for Aquinas) but are such as to allow God some alternatives. If a contemporary ontology stresses the priority of an absolute infinity of possible individuals, then the achievement of Divine simplicity will be more difficult, but it is also all the more necessary. Such an ontology will remain essentially within a rational framework (although various levels may be distinguished), because the distinctions which rational thought needs will remain, and division within Divinity must be prevented in ways more difficult than that of placing God beyond reason's basic distinction (i.e., the distinction of thought and its object).

Plato prevents division and achieves simplicity through harmony or proportion, as accomplished by the self-sustaining activity characteristic of soul, all of which is guided by reference to a realm of Forms themselves more simple and self-sustaining than the world which embodies them. Both Plato and Aristotle represent a compromise and achieve simplicity without resorting to a perfect unity that would demand transcendence. Even more than does Plato, Aristotle uses the limiting qualities of form as characteristic of his unmoved mover, orienting its attention only toward its own actualized thought, since the potentiality inherent in matter is the very epitome of the possibility of division. Plotinus always stands as the champion of an unrestrained demand for unity as the central perfection, with its absolute guarantee of simplicity and the impossibility of division, but also with its necessary transcendence of direct rational grasp. It must not be overlooked that multiplicity is present within the Plotinian One, in the sense that it contains the causes for all intellectual and natural phenomena. But such variety is present without the distinctions which hold entities apart from one another and so could not possibly be a source of division (that is, until this multiplicity becomes structured within the confines of being).

Augustine's God tends to have the simplicity of unchangeableness, although this requires the predestination of the natural order. What cannot change surely cannot fall prey to division, but then neither is any alternative action open to such a God nor in any essential sense to men. Aquinas allows alternative possible worlds to exist in the mind of God but preserves unchangeableness and thus simplicity by making the selection of the possibles in the act of creation a process without alternatives even for a God. "Will" is a more important concept for Thomas because of the presence of these unactualized possibles, but the selection that such a will can achieve is determined for it without alternative. A further guarantee of the Divine simplicity is present in Aquinas' denial that creatures have any real relations with God, although He stands in a relationship of a creator to His creation. What cannot be touched from below cannot possibly be subject to division from any outside force.

With Scotus and Ockham, however, we find more status given to relations, particularly to mutual relations between God and man. For Hegel relations become ultimately real and God cannot even be God without encompassing every possible relationship. Under such conditions simplicity is difficult to maintain, but Hegel does it by making the development of the relations a necessary process, hence incapable of being divided by the freedom of alternative routes. Spinoza's simplicity is similar to this, that is, the simplicity of an absolute infinity which excludes nothing and therefore has nothing outside of itself capable of causing any difficulty. When all can be viewed as necessary and without alternative, then all relations and all entities can be introduced into the Divine life (along with an infinite reason capable of comprehending them), and still there need be no fear of a loss of simplicity via division. This is, to be sure, not the simplicity which strict unity provides but the simplicity of a complex and yet fully realized system. No unrealized possibles can remain and no alternative courses of action can be seen.

With unrealized and non-compossible possible entities, the maintenance of simplicity is more difficult, although a freedom of alternative structures is also more easily achieved. Leaving this issue until the next section, it is still easy to see that simplicity is necessary to Divine perfection (to distinguish its existence from that which depends upon it) but that this simplicity may be achieved in a variety of ways. Moreover, this variety of approaches is possible due to the fact that it is not so much simplicity itself as the lack of potentiality for division (and thus change of nature) which must be prevented. The harmony and proportion of Plato prevent division as successfully as the unity of Plotinus, although in some sense the latter attribute achieves a greater simplicity. The introduction of possible entities into the Divine nature presents a more difficult problem in that other Divine characteristics must now be stressed (e.g., power and will). The possible entities in the Divine mind no longer themselves provide the insurance against division as they did in the days when their actualization was without alternative. To free creative action and yet to preserve Divinity's perfection (self-sufficiency), that is the contemporary ontological problem.

13

FREEDOM

AND VOLITION:

A CONCLUSION

In *The Idea of Perfection in Christian Theology,* R. N. Flew traces the concept of ethical and spiritual perfection through its history within Christian life and writing. In a much more modest fashion, this brief essay has attempted to develop a counterpart to the type of perfection with which Flew has so comprehensively dealt. Although it is not entirely decisive, the ontological concept of Divine perfection certainly has a great deal to do with the formation of any idea of ethical and spiritual perfection. We do not all agree as to what God's perfection is like, and our decisions about Divine perfection will affect the kind of perfection which we deem to be desirable or attainable by man. The latter may be a consideration which comes to our attention prior in time, but Divine perfection is certainly ontologically prior and the more important concept for us to form. The mystical, and even the monastic, life is closely linked to a concept of Divine perfection in which transcendence is stressed. If God did not transcend ordinary categories, the separation from life's common ways would not be necessary and might even be misleading. The spiritual attitude toward prayer, not to mention the ethical attitude of responsibility, are almost entirely dependent upon some view of the Divine freedom and foreknowledge.

Any particular view of the form of the religious life, then, depends for its sanction upon the reference to a particular concept of the Divine perfection. Contrary to popular opinion, in the use of any term which has application to both Divine and natural beings, it is the Divine meaning which is normative and which determines that term's varied employment in human affairs. We may begin with the question of "will" as it relates to man's action, but a conclusion about its proper employment comes only after we have constructed a theory which shows its use in characterizing the Divine nature. To be sure, the Divine employment will differ from the human use of the term, but specifying the difference of its application within the Divine nature will at the same time yield a specification of that word's proper human use. All important concepts (e.g., being, good, will, etc.) have a Divine application, from which alone proper human usage can be determined.

It is not the ordinary but the extraordinary use of language which reveals to us its substance. For the trivial events of life perhaps no Divine reference is necessary. But for most of the important concepts that are applicable to man, the contrast of the Divine with the natural application of the term is helpful. Certainly a language may be worked out along solely naturalistic principles; but, if a concept of Divinity is to be constructed, then one of its major functions ought to be to give precision to terminology through contrasting the Divine nature with all the important human concepts. For example, the central term under consideration here, "freedom," cannot have its boundaries determined until we have decided what freedom means as applicable to the Divine nature. If freedom in God means absolute necessity and also self-determination, then freedom for man can only mean necessity too, coupled however (because he is finite) with a lack of complete self-determination (e.g., Spinoza). God's nature, being as it is the source of our created order, is too determinative to overlook whenever we work out the applicability of terms within the realm of nature.

Does this mean that it is an easy or a simple matter to know God directly? No, all that is implied is that a possible theory of the Divine nature always needs to be constructed. "Possible" in this case is determined by the accumulated criteria provided by the major views of the Divine nature, contrasted with the magnitude of the data in the natural order for which such a Divinity must provide an account. Able to answer classical requirements and able to give an explanation for the form of the natural order—such a theory can be called a possible theory of the Divine nature. In some non-verbalized, spiritual life God may be quite real and singular in nature. All spoken religious life, however, becomes itself a theory, subject to human variation and to the difficulties that any transcendent expression encounters within a linguistic framework (since theories are possible only in terms of words or concepts). Theoretically, the various concepts of Divinity are multiple, and all that we can require of any man is that he be able to demonstrate the possible existence and the possible explanatory usefulness of his concept of the Divine nature.

Since God has no lips He cannot speak, which is another way of saying that every "word of God" must come from human lips. This means that we have much indirect but no direct word about God and by God. Were it otherwise, we would have but one religion and one doctrine of the nature of God. With no direct word available or possible, what can we learn by indirection from the very situation of the multiplicity of the views themselves? Variations in our theories about God indicate the multitude of the possible qualities within the Divine nature which can be variously (i.e., humanly) apprehended. Our only danger is one of limiting God to our particular possible apprehension, thus denying the absolutely infinite extent of the possible entities within the Divine nature. What shall we do to distinguish among conflicting and competing theories and to reject those which might be unacceptable? Here a concept of perfection is a necessary but not a sufficient condition for selection. To serve as an explanatory cause for creation, a Divinity must be shown to embody perfection, although no single set of standards for fixing this concept can be established in advance.

Although this is not the place to point out the limits of the question of how we may distinguish the acceptable from among the unacceptable theories of the Divine nature, it is proper to note the similarity here to Plato's concern in the *Phaedrus*. Not all possession of an individual by passions and psychological forces (e.g., love) is necessarily bad. In fact, some of the greatest blessings come by means of madness, but by a madness which is Divinely inspired. Therefore, all who speak at any length about God are possessed men (since the object of their conversation is outside the natural order), and it is our task not to reject psychological possession by non-natural forces but to try to distinguish that which reveals Divinity from that which results from a demonic possession that is all too frighteningly similar to it. The creative expression of theologically dominated men—that is what the "word of God" means. Such a creative use of words presents a word in a way in which it has not quite been presented to the world before, because such a word now represents the Divine possibles. To assess such an expression means to locate it within the Divine nature, to see what sort of a possible it is within God's life. This is a human word now transposed to its location within the Divine possibles and as such made revelatory of God's nature.

Why as human beings do we write about metaphysics at all? To give definitive formulations to solutions proposed, or to provide the mind with material for consideration? Of necessity it must be the latter, for the creative use of all important terms (i.e., representing them as they exist among the Divine attributes, as the original source of the natural order) itself prevents an exact understanding of these terms solely from their previous usage. The extent of the Divine possibles is itself what allows such a variety of meanings to become attached to terms, since there is nothing in the world which might not have been otherwise. The lack of fixity of an exact meaning to all important terms is an evidence of this fact. All new discourse about God of necessity cannot be simply factual. It gives common terms new meanings to bear. Thus, the creative expression of the Divine nature takes terms of human origin and attempts to alter their meaning to make them suitable to the Divine. Given the perfection of God and the natural incommensurability between our language and such a being, the words used about God are bound to change and bound to change their meaning. We must turn to expressions of past ages for help, but we can never utter exactly the same words again, language and God being what they are.

If we consider the particular concepts at issue here (freedom and volition), the problem we face can be seen clearly. We must come to understand such terms through a study of at least some of their historic uses, but it is obvious that under no conditions can these concepts apply to man and to God in exactly the same way in a new age. A concept of Divine perfection must be constructed to determine what the resulting deficiencies will be if these ordinary terms are applied to God. But to do this means to say a great deal about God when He has said no single direct word about His nature to all of us. What do we do, then? We construct a theory of an absolute infinity of possibles and then of a Divine nature sufficient to encompass them. However, oriented as we now are away from natural objects toward the possibles in the Divine nature, our terms will begin to shift in meaning and in that sense old terms will become novel. The creative process is at work within human language, and the Divine as well as the demonic possessive forces will again need to be distinguished from each other.

As such, "freedom" and "volition" are modern problems. This does not at all mean that classical writers did not consider such concepts. Aristotle specifically states that no action can be considered moral unless it is voluntary. The only uniquely modern characteristic of these concepts is their recent centrality. Freedom and volition used to be considered human qualities within an ontological framework to which the terms could not really be applied. With the introduction of possibles into the Divine nature and their reconciliation with perfection, these two concepts came to have a meaningful application to Divinity and to the ontological framework in general. As long as necessity governed both Divine action and the ontological order, freedom and volition could at best be only minor human problems without a foundation in the natural order itself. The medievals in considering God, and then the moderns in considering nature, in turn become aware of a lack of necessity about the Divine and the natural order. Now freedom and volition have become major issues with an ontological and a Divine application as well as a human one.

Sometimes these modern considerations are posed by asking about "personality," i.e., whether its central characteristics apply to Divinity (or even to nature) in such a way that man's ontological structure is not unique. The nineteenth century took the model for its ontological structure from the self, until the classical problems of transcendence disappeared, and God, nature, and man (and thus the language applicable to all three) became very close in structure. The stress upon human characteristics as ontologically revealing has been continued by existentialism into our own day. What we now need is to recover a sensitivity to classical problems, in which a First Principle could not be spoken about easily, since its structure differed so from our own. The nineteenth century has spent its energy with incredible fruitfulness. Today we require that "freedom" and "volition" receive attention, but this time against a more classical background—we must ask about the appropriateness of their ontological and theological attribution. God, the world, and man need to be seen as contrasting structures. Man will always be temporally prior, but the construction of a theory of Divine perfection ought once again to become ontologically prior and the first order of theological business.

Considering "volition" first, it is evident that both Plato and Aristotle gave it a central place within human nature and made its proper employment (i.e., as rationally trained and guided) the very condition for achieving freedom (i.e., freedom from dominance by passion). Volition in Divinity, however, is another matter. Obviously, for Aristotle such a term could not apply to his unmoved mover, for volition indicates something sought for and thus something lacking in that nature. The unmoved mover's activity of thought is self-sufficient and complete-in-itself, and a will which could produce a volition would actually introduce a defect. Plato is somewhat more complicated. If we take the Forms as the embodiment of perfection, then the incompatibility of volition with perfection is even more obvious than in Aristotle. However, in contrast, it is a different story when we consider "soul," and particularly the "world maker" of the *Timaeus.* Plato obviously applies "volition" to such activity; and yet, in its perfect embodiment, this does not require freedom. The possibility for alternative action is characteristic only of imperfect men; the world maker creates because he is good and not grudging. It takes volition to release his creative power, but his actions have no alternatives open to them. Here is the source for one long-dominant theory of Divine perfection.

With Plotinus and Dionysius the Areopagite the situation is somewhat altered. Soul and its volitional capacities are much more central to perfection than in the usual Aristotelian-derived views. But neither volition nor freedom can really be said to characterize either the One or the super-essential Godhead as such. Creative energy flows from the creative source, but volition is not a characteristic distinct from the objects to which such energy is applied, until we reach a level outside the First Principle. Volition as a power requires a definiteness and a presence of distinction that prevents man from attributing it to his Divinity as a perfection. Freedom can be applied to the First in an interesting way, however, in the sense that it transcends all the bonds and distinctions characteristic of being's structure. The First is thus itself free from all of the restrictions present in the levels created by it, although this is a freedom of the transcendence of rational structure and never the freedom of alternative action. Choice would require the presence of unacceptable distinctions.

Augustine's early picture of perfection seems very close to Roman rational necessity, but in the later writings this becomes modified to include volition and other aspects of personality. Yet the classical restrictions against contingency and change prevent Augustine from ever allowing volition in God to imply any genuine choice among alternatives—at least as rationally knowable. The pattern of the future, Augustine is quite sure, is fixed unchangeably in the Divine knowledge. The outcome of God's activity and the process of nature are clearly embraced in a classical view of essential unalterability. Yet creation *ex nihilo* has altered the picture for Augustine. Time now has a different position within the Divine nature, since God is the source of all that is in time. The power of God is also stressed, which means that the possibility of alternative selection (particularly as regards salvation) becomes real for Augustine. However, the ontological framework Augustine uses is not such as to allow freedom of choice without imperfection, and so the inscrutability of the Divine volition must be postulated. Any scheme of creation and salvation introduces alternatives; but, with a metaphysical framework that cannot deal with them, perfection is preserved by placing the basis for decision beyond human scrutiny and making its outcome fully determined and foreknowable throughout eternity.

Augustine introduced novel problems but did not alter the basic ontological framework. Aquinas subjects the operation of the Divine will in decision to scrutiny, and he finds its selection of alternatives fully rational but also fully determined by other aspects (e.g., goodness) of the Divine nature. Thomas makes the Divine alternatives real; Ockham makes them possible and raises volition to a more central place in Divine perfection. As we progress chronologically, *freedom has been growing in meaning as ontological alternatives have increased.* When volition becomes central to Divinity, then freedom may mean more than an absence of exterior determination. Nevertheless, Spinoza will revert to a more classical view. Such freedom as Ockham postulates subjects the whole order of nature to contingency, although the Divine nature itself is not similarly contingent. Volition present within creation is a source of contingency, although God's own nature is not itself contingent. That is, God is contingent only as including an infinite set of possible individuals, some of which He never selects for inclusion in nature and others of which, although they are definitely real potentials, become dependent upon nature's contingency for their actualization.

Existentialism resembles a form of Hegelianism in its use of personality as the central metaphysical object, yet it is actually the existentialists who have reintroduced a stress upon volition and freedom where Hegelian derived views have been almost classically deterministic. The discovery of genuine alternatives available to human volition has reopened the question of volition as a Divine characteristic, although volition can never be a part of God in exactly the same way that it characterizes men. The existentialists suffer from the modern restrictions against constructive metaphysics and theology, and this constricts their formation of theories about God's nature. Such a speculative task is required, however, in order to disclose the ontological sources of possible human volition. Necessity characterized both knowledge and perfection for Aristotle. To be such that it could not be otherwise was for him the very mark of stability, and volition was a sign of weakness. *The problem, then, is to permit Divine volition without damaging self-sufficiency or power.* If volition is to be attributed to Divinity, necessity cannot characterize the act of creation, although necessity may still be applied to the Divine nature as a whole. Contingency may characterize Divine action, but not the substance of the Divine attributes themselves. In human nature contingency characterizes both action and the instruments of action—that is, man's attributes are themselves contingent in their performance. Here is the basis for the question of attributing "personality" to Divinity. Choice necessarily involves distinctions, and as such these distinctions could not be characteristic of the Plotinian One. Personality is central for Plotinus but not compatible with perfection at its fullest. If personality is to be attributable to Divinity, necessity can no longer characterize Divine action, although the Divine nature always is necessarily what it is in its inclusion of attributes. Choice is based upon volition, which in turn depends upon the presence of distinctions and of a range of possible individual entities in themselves unactualizable but out of which the Divine selection is made. Personality in this sense is perhaps attributable to Divinity without involving the defects so characteristic of human personality.

14

EXTENSION

OF

CONCLUSIONS

If the thesis of this essay is true, then "perfection" is the most important concept in establishing a view of the Divine nature and in determining man's relationship to that First Principle, both in nature and in knowledge. If "freedom" provides a more contemporary perspective on perfection, and if freedom is determined by the way in which "volition" is to be attributed, then what happens to the other central terms relating to perfection (infinity and unity, form and transcendence, self-sufficiency and actuality, power and motion, simplicity and division) when freedom becomes the central issue? Obviously, there is no one, single way to specify Divine perfection. These twelve concepts (freedom and volition, plus the ten listed directly above) tend to be the ones which cluster around the classical definitions, interrelated in a way that involves the definition of all of the others in the specification of the use of any one term.

Certain metaphysical views about the nature and origin of the natural order influence our choice of which terms are most important. We can indicate possible views of perfection and the advantages and disadvantages which accompany each concept. We can never fix on a single view as alone being adequate, although the historical writings help us to see what a concept of perfection must include if it is to become available for theological use.

An ability to eliminate inadequate views (i.e., ones which are not capable of sustaining the Divine life internally) but not to fix on any single view or even to limit the number of possible views of perfection is, as pointed out above, a revealing fact both about the Divine life and about human language. The more important the concept, the more language becomes subject to variation and the more obvious becomes our inherent inability to fix a single meaning for the term. Thus, every new discourse about Divinity will evidence this flexibility of meaning which language exhibits whenever it concerns God. In turn, this tells us something about God: His nature is such that it contains the unlimited number of possibles to which our unending discourse is a painful testimony. The prosaic and unimportant details of human life can be expressed simply and in final form. However, the more complex aspects of existence begin to evidence the same basic involvement in an indefinitely extended possibility that appears when we approach Divinity. God has no need to speak about Himself, but when men use their only tools, words, their unending speech proclaims their involvement in an absolute infinity of possibles which only a perfect Divinity could control with success.

Infinity, it is easy to see, is important for any concept of perfection which takes as its starting point the question of freedom. If the world is limited in possibility, human freedom may still be attainable but human creativity will be somewhat restricted. If infinity does not apply to God, then He has no alternatives to work with, since our finite series would be the only candidate for actualization. When infinity applies to God, as freedom seems to demand (particularly if it is an absolute infinity of kinds), then infinity becomes a central

Divine attribute and requires the involvement of possibility in the Divine nature, if all of such possibles are not capable of eventual actualization. An infinite time span need not admit such full actualization, although it does as Spinoza conceives of it, but the limited time span required by a doctrine of creation means that a choice from among possibles becomes a necessity. From here on it is the details of accounting for this choice which determine whether freedom is central to perfection, or whether necessity is preserved in the face of infinite possibles by making the process of selection itself necessary.

Unity will necessarily receive a less than dominant place among the Divine attributes, if we begin with freedom as the central concept. Freedom requires choice and choice depends upon alternatives, and successful choice can only take place when the alternative possibles remain clearly distinct. Freedom thus prevents the extreme transcendence of reason which unity taken alone might demand. Nothing is per se beyond rational grasp, since freedom cannot become irrational choice for God as it can for men. Unity still involves transcendence of a kind, since it requires that the Divine intellect be such as to grasp simultaneously all possible entities for consideration. Our intellect would only destroy itself by attempting such a feat. Man's intellect shares infinity in the sense that it is actually applicable to the whole range of possibles, although at any given moment it considers only some perceived finite group. Infinity is not alien to our intellect and does not impede its operation. It speeds the creative process, but it also prohibits our desire to achieve a definiteness not subject to alteration. Lacking the infinite power of Divinity, we still face His intellectual task, and this discrepancy is the source of both our creative powers and our intellectual despair.

Form can be made compatible with infinity, even an absolute infinity of kinds, if the intellect applicable to them is itself actually infinite. This is the argument from the infinite extent of possibility to the infinity of the intellect comprehending them. Man's intellect, although applicable, does not simultaneously grasp the whole range—which distinguishes man from God and indicates why for men infinity often seems indefinite and may appear to lack form. Man's intellect is applicable to a wider range than Aristotle could see, but its limited grasp at any instant always makes the unlimited range open to it seem from a distance to be formless. Freedom requires that form not be transcended, since form is a requirement for rational choice. A Divinity bound by necessity can transcend form and still cause form to be present in a lower order. But a Divinity which must choose freely what that order is to be cannot operate where form is absent. Thus, freedom demands the ultimate maintenance of form in the Divine nature, although never any single form or set of forms.

Transcendence is neither the transcendence of form nor of distinctions. It is the inaccessibility to immediate grasp of all of the infinite possibles. Men transcend their immediate environment, and the provincial terms of their language, when they try to determine what possibles remain, either as potentials within their presently actualized structure or as alternatives to that original structure itself. Creative imagination goes even beyond the bounds of the actualized order to explore possibles as God Himself explores them eternally, as alternatives to the various parts of our order and even to the natural order itself. God transcends our grasp, as holding within His intellect in consideration all possibles simultaneously, although some of the actualizing process is now left to nature and to human will. The Divine nature is transcendent in that it stands behind creation as its cause, the primal creative process of choice itself erecting a barrier which man can guess about (in Plato's phrase construct "likely tales") but never transcend. Whatever we discern about God may be expressed. Language is not transcended, although the possibility of final statement is.

Self-Sufficiency is the main problem that a theory which begins with freedom must face. For freedom in man is often the very evidence of his deficiency in this respect. Lack of stability in internal structure, failure to maintain a decision to actualize—these form a large part of man's freedom, but they also represent his imperfection most dramatically. Thus, from the human side, it is easy to see why self-sufficiency has been preserved as the core of Divine perfection, although it has been maintained through various means. Yet freedom need not be ultimately incompatible with perfection, although self-sufficiency will be the shared characteristic which is least applicable to man and most applicable to God. Change is not even incompatible with self-sufficiency, although it is perhaps the most dangerous characteristic for man. *Control* is the key to the maintenance of self-sufficiency, so that freedom as applied to God must be construed so as to preserve perfect control, an attribute absolutely essential to a creator who is to be the single First Principle.

Actuality will then become the continual actuality of self-sufficiency, not necessarily the absence of change or lack of motion. Of course, actuality can no longer mean that every possible is slated for concrete realization, or else Divine freedom has no area of operation. In this sense, potentiality remains within Divinity, but it is a self-selected potentiality and stands in contrast to a fully organic and self-sustaining natural order. Divine self-sufficiency need not be construed so as to depend upon a full actualization of all possibles; thus freedom of choice can be preserved without destroying perfection. The material processes of the world can be viewed as having their origin in Divine creation, as being from His own nature without involving Him necessarily in the difficulties of potentiality. The created order exists outside the Divine nature, and a perfect and infinite intellect is able to comprehend every aspect of the natural order without difficulty. Like most classical perfections, actuality must be maintained as a Divine perfection, even if not in the specific form of any particular classical view.

Power becomes perhaps the attribute most central to a concept of perfection which begins by considering freedom. For it is power, so to speak, that holds the Divine nature together. When unity is central, nothing needs to be held together. When possibility is either limited or fully actualized, there is no chance of disruptive conflict. But when possibility is absolutely infinite and the Divine attributes are made multiple, then power is crucial and must be absolutely infinite in its extent. Here is perhaps the most dramatic distinction between God and man. Although never comprehending, man's intellect is actually applicable to the full range of the infinite possibles present to God; but the powers of men, although they vary in degree, are never other than finite. This imbalance between degree of power and range of intellectual grasp is the source of most (but by no means all) human evil. Power in God as fully infinite is expressed in the actual selective act of His will, completely adequate to actualize all possibles, although not all simultaneously. Human nature falters, not only in sometimes failing to recognize incompatibles, but in desiring more possibles than are within its own grasp or power to actualize.

Motion must be present whenever power expresses freedom. Human motion sometimes attains its end and sometimes fails, if its power is not sufficient to sustain it. Motion is, then, quite compatible with Divine perfection if the range of power present is always capable of supporting any decision without contingency, which in God's case requires an absolutely infinite power. Motion, however, is still not a primary characteristic of God as it is of man, although it will be possible to Him. Motion was required for the creative act; and, in a religious view, it would be required again for any miracle, a miracle being a kind of partial re-creation of the natural order. Any Divine intervention or appearance, and certainly the process of ending or of transforming the life of the natural order or of an individual, all would require motion. But the continued life of the Divine excludes the variety and constant motion that is so characteristic of less perfect orders.

Simplicity must also be preserved, by means of control via power, in any concept of perfection based upon freedom. Unity and necessity classically were responsible for this important characteristic, but in the face of the absolute infinity of possibles such a desirable goal can still be achieved by power. Human life, carried out as it is among a limited range of possibles, is subject to complexity largely due to our failure to actualize or to maintain a choice once actualized. Divinity does not suffer from this same limitation of power, although the kind of simplicity which infinite power constantly maintains is not the lack of distinction and of alternatives which classical views often demanded. The simplicity here is one of constantly maintained choice. The actualization of possibles did not have to occur as it did, but the element of absolute certainty involved in the process is that of knowing that any choice will be perfectly sustained by an application of infinite power. Simplicity here is the simplicity of the changelessness of a Divine decision.

Division is thus not possible within Divinity, whereas men are sometimes as much divided after a decision as they were before and during the selective process. Traditionally self-sufficiency, unity, and lack of motion were all aimed at removing from the Divine nature any possibility of division. Now the presence of distinction, particularly in the sense of non-compossible possibles, would seem to make division possible, the most unacceptable situation for Divinity which a classical writer could imagine. Although it must be asserted in one sense that such a division within God is possible for a view which makes freedom basic, it must at the same time be said that such a possibility is incapable of being realized, due to the constant preserving bond of Divinity's absolutely infinite power. *The basis for division is present within God, but its actualization is of necessity constantly prevented.* That is one thing which makes God to be God and sets him forever apart from human failure.

The basic sets of concepts necessary for perfection have now been constructed in outline around a concept of freedom. What can be said about some of the other questions which are so often related to the concept of Divine perfection? "Will" perhaps needs little comment, since volition and power are the two components which constitute will. What will is depends upon the power available and the direction and consistency of volition. As these go, so goes will. The question of "foreknowledge" perhaps requires a greater extension of the basic concepts developed here. There is no individual possible entity not directly and eternally present within the Divine nature and not constantly in that intellect's apprehension. The extent of these possibles is absolutely infinite, but so is the range of the Divine intellect. No possible as concretely embodied in the natural order is "within" the Divine nature, although it is still within the range of the Divine intellect and power (which are extended outside Himself in any act of creation or in any miracle). No possible entity within the Divine intellect as such is subject to change, but some receive no concrete embodiment and others depend upon the contingencies of human actualization. Nothing is per se new to God, since no possibles are outside of his constant grasp, but the concrete decisions of human agents are grasped concretely only as actualized in time. God's internal knowledge never changes; His information about the creation existing outside of Him does change in detail but never in general outline or as introducing any unforeseen possibilities.

"Being" is ultimately applicable to God, or else freedom could not be basic to perfection. Being includes the range of the infinite possibles and the other essentials of the Divine nature, i.e., volition, power, intellect and the possible standards for goodness. Being as applied to the created natural order includes these same five basic attributes, but now applied to an actualized finite group. Because these attributes exist primarily in an infinite mode and are actualized as finite only by an act of power and volition (will), aspects of infinity are everywhere present within the natural order. This is particularly so in the areas of volition and intellect, where we find no actual boundaries definitely marking them off from their infinite origin. Power and goodness bear much more clearly the marks of the necessary finite range open to created beings.

"Non-being" derives its principal meaning from the self-contradictory possibles, which are not as such present within the Divine intellect in actual apprehension but are present by negation. Every entity has within itself a relation to a version of itself containing self-contradiction, into which it is always possible for it to fall and to lose that measure of its present being. Other than the ever present self-contradictory counterparts of each possible entity, non-being is present within being in the traditional Platonic form of "otherness." To be what each entity is (including God) it must also be not-every-other-possible-entity (just as it must be not-its-self-contradictory-counterpart). In these two senses non-being is inescapably present within Divinity and within each possible being; and, since possible negative relations are infinite, non-being is present to each finite entity to an infinite degree. The Divine power, being itself absolutely infinite, in its own life keeps such non-being within perfect control. With no such range of power available to sustain us, and with a natural tendency toward both positive and negative infinity within each actual entity, what is amazing is the extent of balance actually achieved in the created order. The considerable lapse toward non-being, or the indefiniteness (for the creature) of infinity about which we are constantly aware, is in fact not nearly so startling as the possibility of achieving even temporary balance.

"Chaos" enters the natural realm as a normal part of its existence. It reflects no similar lack of order in the Divine life but rather the inability of a creature with limited power to resist the constant temptations of infinite desires or the tendency to lapse into non-being, whether intentionally or not. Power had to be granted at the instant of creation sufficient to preserve a basic order and the possibility for order within human affairs. *But the discrepancy between this necessarily finite power and our openness to infinity means that our limited power can fail and chaos can replace order.* Partly this represents the possibility of our actualizing any one of several orders. Indecision, not always a deficiency of power, can often be the cause of chaos. The potentials which result in our chaos are certainly within the Divine nature, but His power coupled with His steady volition and range of knowledge keeps chaos ordered in a manner that is not available to human beings.

"Good" and "evil" are perhaps the most difficult concepts to handle, and therefore they are a testing ground for every metaphysical theory. Metaphysics is never born in ethics (although the desire to use its explaining power may be), but it is here that it often receives its test. Good vs. evil is the most pressing and persistent layman's problem. *If freedom is to be the starting point, then standards of value must be ultimately multiple.* However, since they cannot be standards if they equal in number the entities to be judged, the standards of value themselves must be less than absolutely infinite.

Following Plato's maxim in the *Parmenides,* we would then do well to accept some definite number of possible standards, although we are always powerless to say exactly what number. Standards are not indefinitely numerous, but they are multiple, which accounts for our lack of agreement in ethical theory. Conduct is subject to variation according to the standards men actually select to embody in their practice. God's selection of entities in creation eliminated some standards and perhaps gave us an inclination toward certain others, but only a similarity of standards is possible among men, never an identity. This is as far as the abstract analysis can go; in order to be specific, value theory must turn and deal with the facts of each concrete life.

God's choice in creation was actually subject to much the same conditions. No single standard for goodness binds either Him or His action in creation, although His nature is such as can easily accommodate all of the finite number of possible standards. Being Himself good, God was bound to recognize some, but not all, value standards in creation. Thus, His action remained essentially free, although it was restricted to a finite number of possible combinations involving certain sets of standards. His creation was in that sense good, although it was not necessary, and it was not by any means the only possible combination of value standards. Since possible standards are always multiple and lack the rigid necessity of singularity, it is always possible for men to hold to a selected set of standards or to violate values at any time, often in the name of other values. Hence the presence of "evil" (plus the limitations on power, volition, and intellect previously described), and such is its source in a Divine nature not itself ever actually evil.

The ascription of "positive attributes" to Divinity is, quite obviously, always possible within this theory. Negative procedures, however, are still necessary in that no attribute can be given to God without first distinguishing between God and creatures and then denying of the term the aspects which are found to be inapplicable to God. No term, deriving as it does from our normal language, is applicable directly to God without first applying a negative procedure, which in turn depends upon a theory of the Divine perfection. The establishment of this theory, which is to become the standard for negation, itself depends upon first denying of Divinity any aspect which would render it incapable of its actual act, i.e., creation and its maintenance. The possibility of positive attribution does not necessarily mean that this theory asserts that God is easily knowable. Before very much can be done in the way of construction, a whole philosophical and theological tradition must be mastered. However, a theory of perfection which is constructed around freedom does remove many of the insuperable obstacles to direct knowledge that are present in many traditional theories.

Since positive attribution is at least possible, even if it cannot be absolutely definitive, such a theory has an obvious kinship to the method of univocity. Equivocity is associated with a theory of perfection which involves extreme transcendence, and analogy is a special and controversial view which tries to preserve a ground for knowledge even when the object is agreed to be above direct grasp. As ought to be obvious, nothing could be more futile than arguing for a theory of language which uses terms for Divine attribution as univocal. The issue lies not in language or in our use of terms but in the theory we construct about the Divine nature and the mode of knowledge applicable to such a nature. When the concept of Divine perfection is worked out, then it will always be easy to see in what sense ordinary terms may be appropriated.

What is to be concluded? What we have arrived at after much difficult consideration is not God Himself, but merely one theory about God which we can assert with confidence to be fully possible. It is not the business of metaphysics to decide among such possible concepts as still remain. It may guide the theologian to the promised land of usable concepts, but it is forbidden to any metaphysician to decide upon the precise place and moment of the Divine entry into the possibles, which knowledge alone could yield a single, incontrovertible theory of both nature and the Divine nature. To outline and to work within a limited number of possible theories—such is man's intellectual and moral limit and his required task.

SELECTED READINGS

CHAPTER I

Plato: *Laws,* Bk. X; *Parmenides; Phaedrus,* 245C–256E; *Philebus,* 58C–67B; *Republic,* 376E–392C and 502C–509C; *Sophist; Timaeus,* 27–54.

Aristotle: *Generation and Corruption; Metaphysics,* Bk. Lambda; *Nicomachean Ethics,* Bk. X; *Physics,* Bks. III, VIII.

CHAPTER II

Plotinus: *Enneads* (See especially the treatises of the Fifth and Sixth Enneads, and I.8 and III.2.)

Dionysius the Areopagite: *The Divine Names; Mystical Theology.*

CHAPTER III

Augustine: *The Trinity,* Books I, III, V, VI, XV; *Concerning the Nature of the Good; Confessions,* Books XI and XII; *Divine Providence and the Problem of Evil; Enchiridion; Free Will; Grace and Free Will.*

Anselm: *Monologium,* Chs. I–XXVII; *Appendix in Behalf of the Fool; Proslogium.*

CHAPTER IV

Thomas Aquinas: *Summa Theologica,* Part I, QQ. 2–49; *Summa Contra Gentiles,* Bk. I.

William of Ockham: *Philosophical Writings,* ed. P. Boehner, Chs. VII–X; *Studies and Selections,* ed. S. C. Tornay, "On the Ideas of God."

Duns Scotus: *De Primo Principio.*

CHAPTER V

Meister Eckhart: "About Disinterest"; "Talks of Instruction;" and selected Sermons.

Nicolas Cusanus: *Learned Ignorance,* Bk. I.

CHAPTER VI

Spinoza: *Ethics,* Part I; *Cognitata Metaphysica; Principles of Descartes' Philosophy,* Pt. I; *Tractatus Theologico-Politicus.*

Leibniz: *Theodicy,* Part I; *Discourse on Metaphysics,* I–XVI; *Monadology,* 31–90; *The Ultimate Origination of Things.*

CHAPTER VII

Kant: *Critique of Pure Reason,* "Transcendental Dialectic"; *Critique of Aesthetic Judgement,* "Analytic of the Sublime"; *Religion Within the Limits of Reason Alone.*

Hegel: *Phenomenology of Mind,* "Revealed Religion" and "Absolute Knowledge"; *Early Theological Writings,* Trans. Knox and Kroner; *Lectures on the Philosophy of Religion.*

ADDITIONAL SOURCES

Barth, Karl. *Church Dogmatics,* Vol. II, part 1: *The Doctrine of God.* New York, Charles Scribner's Sons.

Bergson, Henri. *Creative Evolution.* Modern Library ed. New York, Random House, 1944.

Bonaventura. *Breviloquim.* Trans. E. E. Nemmers. St. Louis, B. Herder Book Co., 1946.

Bolzano, Bernard. *Paradoxes of the Infinite.* Trans. Donald A. Steele. New Haven, Yale University Press, 1950.

Brunner, H. Emil. *The Christian Doctrine of God (Dogmatics,* Vol. I). Philadelphia, Westminster Press, 1950.

Farrer, Austin. *Finite and Infinite.* Westminster, London, Dacre Press, 1943.

———. *The Freedom of the Will.* London, A. & C. Black, 1958.

Flew, Robert Newton. *The Idea of Perfection in Christian Theology.* London, H. Milford, Oxford University Press, 1934.

Foss, Martin. *The Idea of Perfection in the Western World.* Princeton, Princeton University Press, 1946.

Garrigou-Lagrange, Reginald. *Christian Perfection and Contemplation.* St. Louis, B. Herder Book Co., 1937.

Hartshorne, Charles. *The Divine Relativity.* New Haven, Yale University Press, 1948.

———. *Man's Vision of God.* Chicago, Willett, Clark & Co., 1941.

———. *The Logic of Perfection.* LaSalle, Ill., Open Court Publishing Co. (in preparation).

Heidegger, Martin. *Being and Time.* Trans. John Macquarrie and Edward Robinson, New York, Harper and Brothers, 1962.

Philo Judaeus. *The Unchangeableness of God* and *The Account of the World's Creation.* In *Philosophical Works.* Loeb Classical Library ed. Cambridge, Harvard University Press.

Temple, William. *Nature, Man and God.* New York, St. Martin's Press, 1953. Part I.

Tillich, Paul. *Systematic Theology.* Chicago, University of Chicago Press, 1951. Vol. I.

Weiss, Paul. *Modes of Being.* Carbondale, Southern Illinois University Press, 1958.

Whitehead, Alfred North. *Process and Reality.* New York, Humanities Press, 1957. Part V.

INDEX